HARRIER

JUMP JET INTERDICTION

STEVE STONE

© Steve Stone 2015

Steve Stone has asserted his rights under the Copyright, Design and Patents Act, 1988, to be identified as the author of this work.

Published by Digital Dream Publishing 2015

ISBN-13: 978-1539479208

ISBN-10: 153947920X

Contents

AUTHOR'S NOTE 4
PROLOGUE 6
CHAPTER ONE - KABUL 16
CHAPTER TWO - JTAC 21
CHAPTER THREE – HARRIER INCEPTION 26
CHAPTER FOUR – INSURGENT HUNT 33
CHAPTER FIVE – PEGASUS ENGINE 41
CHAPTER SIX – HELMAND HORROR 48
CHAPTER SEVEN – SPECIAL BOAT SERVICE 56
CHAPTER EIGHT – CAMP BASTIAN 61
CHAPTER NINE – SEA HARRIER 69
CHAPTER TEN – RECOIL SIX 77
CHAPTER ELEVEN – JOINT FORCE HARRIER 81
CHAPTER TWELVE – AV-8B 85
CHAPTER THIRTEEN – STORMY WEATHER 89
CHAPTER FOURTEEN – FINAL BOW 97
GLOSSARY 103
APPENDIX – HISTORY OF ZG477 114

AUTHOR'S NOTE

The Harrier has a unique place in aviation history as the most successful VTOL aircraft to date. Born from the need during the Cold War for an aircraft that could operate even if airfields had been destroyed. The Harrier has become yet another British aviation icon alongside the Spitfire and Concord. Under a small but outstanding team under designer Sir Sydney Camm designer of Hawker Hurricane fame along with Sir Stanley Hooker Bristol's Technical Director led to the P.1127 forerunner to the Harrier. Such was its success that it was also built under licence in America by McDonnell Douglas (now Boeing) and the Americans along with the British aided in improving it for both later American (AV-8B) and British (GR5, GR7, GR9) versions. The Harrier has fought in several theatres including the Falklands, former Yugoslavia, Iraq and Afghanistan. Roving its value time and time again as a formidable fighter bomber.

Now retired from British service with both the Royal Navy and RAF, it is still very much active with the U.S Marine Corps until ultimately being replaced by the Lockheed Martin F-35B STOVL (short takeoff and vertical landing). The F-35B will start to replace the AV-8B in 2016, but the AV-8B will continue in service until 2025. Meanwhile, the AV-8B will receive revamped defensive measures, updated data-link capability and targeting sensors, and improved missiles, among other enhancements. This unique book looks not only at the amazing history of the Harrier, but follows Harrier GR9A ZG477 into active duty in Afghanistan for its last combat operations with the RAF in 2009. Fighting a deadly and tenacious foe showing no fear towards coalition forces.

PROLOGUE

August 2008

I walked out to the flight line, where my Harrier, a GR9A ZG477 was waiting. ZG477 was originally built as a GR7 as part of a batch of 34 delivered in August 1990. The GR7 having been in service since 1990 with the RAF and has been operationally deployed in the Gulf, the Balkans, Sierra Leone, Iraq and now Afghanistan. The GR9 is essentially a GR7 upgraded by BAE Systems to the GR9 standard. Which included improved weapon-aiming systems and improved navigation, and also added new weapons to our arsenal. In January 2007 two GR9s were deployed to Afghanistan as part of NATO International Security Force (ISAF).

My G-suit pockets were filled with maps, even though the Harrier had its own built in maps – which used GPS signals for a precise location. Although the electronic aids added to the GR9 are still way short of the Typhoon. The Harrier though, tests your piloting kills each and every time you strap yourself in. It is an aircraft that demands respect. The AV-8A Harrier and its successor, the AV-8B, have been in 143 major non-combat accidents, killing 45 Marine pilots. The UK had nearly 90 non-combat accidents for all versions of Harriers during their service, excluding prototypes.

As part of Operation Herrick from July 2008 to July 2009. Eight Harriers were continuously available in theatre, with missions flown in pairs, two pairs on day tasking's and one pair at night, with other aircraft on alert during the day. Our main area of operations was over the Helmand Valley, 15-20 minutes flying time from Kandahar, supporting the British Army along with the Royal Marines and other coalition troops. Other areas we covered included the Khyber Pass and Pakistan, Iran, Turkmenistan and Uzbekistan border regions.

This was my first sortie in the 'Stan.' I could feel the hot late morning sun on my back, as I walked along a dusty cracked path past some hangers, empty apart from a C-17 undergoing maintenance. Our Harriers were awaiting our arrival on the flight line. The ground crew still scurrying around them, making final preparations. With a final walk round my aircraft, and final checks, including checking the master armament safety switch. It was time to climb board and start the Rolls Royce Pegasus engine. After checking the various switches in the cockpit were in the right position, I clicked the ignition button on the throttle lever. I could hear the igniter click before a light wine from the engine and a cloud of black smoke emanating from the rear - this was soon replaced with a roar as the Pegasus engine came up to idle. A slight nudge of the throttle was all that was needed to get the Harrier rolling. We moved off the flight line and onto the taxiway for the short run to the runway. The concrete on the taxiway was crumbling, some areas worse than others. It was said that the reverse thrust from the C-17 Globemaster, used to reverse them from their hard standing and onto the taxiway had exasperated the damage. The runway had been fully re-surfaced, though, shortly after Kandahar had been captured in 2001.

We were cleared for takeoff and whilst making our way to the runway, we completed all the pre-takeoff checks before turning onto the runway and winding our engines up. The lead Harrier released its brakes and roared off down the runway in a cloud of dust and smoke before climbing into the bright blue sky.

It was my turn next. I pushed e throttle lever fully forward and was pushed back in my ejection seat as all 23,400lb of thrust from the MK107 Pegasus engine pushed me down the runway. The aircraft rocked back and forth as the speed built up to 140 knots. I pulled the lever to angle the jet nozzles downward slightly and the Harrier jumped into the air, quickly building up speed to 400 knots as I climbed into the morning sky. I quickly retracted the landing gear, flaps and pointing the engine nozzles fully rearward. With a full fuel tank and ordnance the Harrier did not have the same nimbleness and my stick moves needed to be more progressive. It felt as if I was driving a bus instead of a sports car. When fully fuelled, with 11,700lb of fuel, this would give us over two hours of flight time without the need of mid-air refuelling.

With the mid-air or air-to-air refuelling capability, our time on station could be dramatically increased, with some missions lasting well over six hours. The tactical climb to 10,000 feet was always the most worrying - constantly looking at the three rear view mirrors for any sign of a missile attack. The GR9 cockpit itself is very busy with two TVs displaying anything from Sniper imagery, through to weapon programming, engine performance data or a moving map. We also could simultaneously make use of two radios to keep in contact with the ground forces, wingman or other various agencies that help make the tactical decisions.

At 20,000 feet, I joined the lead Harrier and joined him in a wingtip formation. Below us was Afghanistan's almost stark terrain, which looked so peaceful, yet deadly. We began our patrol in earnest, however, everything could change in seconds in Afghanistan. Our role included that of close support, which meant we could be called in to support troops at any moment. Flying around, we were an emergency service to coalition troops, swooping in and letting off a few rockets or dropping a few bombs, before swooping off to another target or back home.

Just 20 minutes into the flight, our first call came in from JTAC, "Jaguar Zero One, Recoil Six Four. Recoil Six Four, Jaguar Zero One. Over the secure radio we didn't need to use codes. Jaguar Zero One simply needed to tell us what our mission was. Our mission was a variation of the usual close support that saw us on average drop around 1000lbs of bombs a day.

This mission was to offer close support to some Royal Marines working alongside the Afghan National Army. They were being pinned down by a Taliban position cross one of the many irrigation canals scattered throughout Helmand. The nearest friendly ground forces were three clicks away and it was our job to suppress the position. Obliterate if at all possible. JTAC continued to pass on attack data and relay information from the eyes on the ground. As with any close support mission, our first priority was to ensure we avoided any blue on blue. At times the type of ordnance we could use depended on friendly positions. The higher the yield of a weapon the larger the blast radius. The weapon with the smallest yield we carried was the CRV7 rockets mounted on a pod, on a wing hardpoint. The CRV7, short for "Canadian Rocket Vehicle 7", is a folding-fin ground attack rocket produced by Bristol Aerospace in Winnipeg, Manitoba. It was first introduced in the early 1970s as an upgraded version of the standard U.S. 2.75 inch air-to-ground rockets. The CRV7 still remains one of the most powerful air-to-ground attack rockets to this day, and has slowly become the de facto standard for Western forces outside the United States. The pod carried on the Harrier contains 19 individual rockets; giving a total of 38. The

CRV7 is a good replacement for a gun. We can select whether or not to fire one rocket, 38 rockets or any multiple in between. The friendly position was a Royal Marines patrol who had already stated that ammunition was running low, which heightened the urgency for close air support. Our target was not too difficult to find once we had eyes on the right stretch of canal. The Royal Marines stated they were receiving heavy as well as light machine gun fire from a position to their one o'clock. Before our first run, I double checked the Royal Marines position before lying down any fire. In a fast paced dynamic close attack is all too easy to cause a blue on blue.

I jinked left and looked out of the canopy before looking down to my instruments and performed a hard left hand turn which pushed me down into my ejection seat and the bellows of my G-suit inflated around my legs. I could see the friendly position and the enemy position on the top of a small hill surrounded by trees with thick vegetation. It was a commanding position and the Taliban must have known that. I knew as well as performing an attack I had to keep my eye open for any surface to air weapons, which could ruin a good day.

The Taliban was putting down such a large amount of fire, that neither the Royal Marines or Afghan Army could even make a tactical withdrawal. This was the main reason along with becoming low on ammunition that they had called in air support.

JTAC are the ones that make all the decisions, though we are simply an asset and are told what weapon would be the best or a particular target. For a soft target like the Taliban out in the open, rockets would suffice initially. We had 540lb airburst bombs which were also highly effective against soft or even slightly hard targets such as dugouts with light to medium overhead protection.

I nudged the stick and with a slight bit of rudder I was lined up and racing towards the target. As I got close, I let off a salvo of rockets. A trail of fiery smoke shot out in front of me as the rockets made their way to the target. Hitting it square on and sending a series of orange and yellow dust clouds shooting into the sky. Almost instantly, firing from the Taliban position was greatly subdued. At the same time a second position opened up just to the right of the first. More than likely some of the Taliban had heard us coming and quickly relocated, pre-empting our attack.

Lt Bob Fox (Fuzz), my wingman made a hard left turn and pulled round to the rear of the position before letting off a salvo of rockets. Hitting the bullseye and quelling the second position. The Marines and Afghan Army started to push forward and cross the road bridge over the canal to the base of the hill - holding short of the Taliban position. Some sporadic small arms fire remained, most likely as the Taliban made a hasty retreat, they were covering their rear.

I was requested to pass over a couple of times and confirm the position was clear. The GR7 and later GR9 was fitted with the Lockheed Martin Sniper or the Selex TIALD 500 targeting pod on the GR7. The improved pod enables us to find and identify groups or individual hostile soldiers in difficult terrain, for example small groups of insurgents in mountainous countryside. The high-resolution optics in the Sniper allow us to also to detect, recognise and identify weapon caches and individuals carrying weapons while remaining beyond jet noise ranges.

The Sniper Advance Targeting Pod (ATP) replaced the TIALD 500 on the GR9 and offered a huge leap forward in capability. Essentially, SNIPER allows us to view the ground from altitude and standoff with incredible resolution for both TV and infrared. This allowed us to operate as well at night as in the day. With the ability to zoom, the pilot had the potential to observe persons on the ground and in some cases, even distinguish between adults and children. Other enhancements on the pod allowed the pilot to generate GPS coordinates from what they are viewing or fire a laser to guide bombs to their point of impact. At night, an infrared pointer allowed the aircraft to operate together and point out ground features to each other. The final addition was that we were able to broadcast the image we saw directly to the soldier on the ground or back to the operations centre. This is crucial when having to make quick tactical decisions. All of this imagery was also recorded for analysis after the mission.

The TERMA pod was a new addition to the Harrier in Afghanistan and provided us with many more defensive flares than the usual internal load; it also provided a missile launch warning to the pilot. The GR9 made its first flight in May 2003 and was accepted into service in September 2006. The in-service date was defined as 24 operationally capable GR9 and one T-12. The remaining 45 aircraft were delivered through to 2009. The GR9A was upgraded with more powerful engines the Pegasus Mk 107 to enable them to perform better in extremely hot climates, which degrade the performance of the existing Pegasus Mk105 turbofan.

This final Taliban position turned out to be clear - the next issue for the boots on the ground would be to ensure that the Taliban had not left any nasty surprises in the form of IEDs to the position they had just vacated. With our fuel level not far from 'bingo' and 'Winchestered' (out of weapons) it was time for us to get back to Kandahar to refuel and rearm. The worst part was always having to leave not knowing if the troops we had just assisted were now safe. More air support if available could be called in. I knew we had left the area with it pretty much clear of enemy forces. But you do sometimes wonder what happened next. On the odd occasion I have bumped into troops we have offered close air support to. When they know who you are, greet you like long lost friends. That little bit of recognition makes it all the more worthwhile. As sometimes at 20,000 feet you do feel detached from the fierce combat on the ground, even if the concern about SAMs is ever present.

CHAPTER ONE - KABUL

A week earlier

A slight bump from the VC-10 as it landed, announced our arrival at Kabul Airport. Having taken off from Brize Norton a few hours earlier. Once at Kabul Airport, after processing, it was then time for a noisy ride aboard a C-130 for the trip to Kandahar Airbase. The webbing seats offered no comfort whatsoever. The stripped out metal interior made for a large echo chamber, in which to reverberate all the noise from the four turboprop engines. As we drew close to the airport, we had to don our helmets and flak jackets in preparation for a tactical decent. A tactical descent was quite simply a steep dive before landing, giving the aircraft the least amount of exposure possible to SAMs. Only twenty four hours ago, I was finishing packing at RAF Cottersmore in Rutland, about to make my way to Brize Norton in Oxfordshire. From the pouring rain and chilly winds, I was now in 35 degree Afghan heat at Kandahar Airbase. Although, the temperature extremes were like going from inside a freezer fridge to a hot oven in a matter of hours. I now had seven years of service flying with the RAF, I suppose more if you want to include my air cadet service prior to joining as a pilot. I have always wanted to fly and my time in the Air Cadets helped me to not only gain my glider pilot's wings but also got me ready for service life. Which is very different to being on civy street. I love the lifestyle and at the moment could not even see myself even thinking about doing anything else. Every time I strapped myself into a Harrier, I know how damn lucky I am; but at the same time how hard, I have had to work to get to where I am now. Kandahar Airbase is located roughly 10 miles southeast of Kandahar City in an almost desolate area, which is essentially a flat plain surrounded by desert. There are mountains to the south on the border with Pakistan, to the south west is Lashkar Ghar the capital of Helmand Province. The airbase occupies a vast space and is the main NATO military hub for operations in southern Afghanistan. The airbase is Afghanistan's second main international airport after Kabul and one of the largest military bases, capable of housing around two hundred military aircraft. The airport was originally built in the 1960s by the Afghan government. The Soviets occupied the airbase during the 1980 Soviet war in Afghanistan. After the Soviet withdrawal the airport remained in control of Najibullah's government until he stepped down in 1992. Local warlord Gul Agha Sherzai was in charge of the airport until the Taliban took control of Kandahar in 1994. They were driven out of the country during Operation Enduring Freedom in late 2001. The airport was damaged by U.S. and British bombings in October 2001.

In 2007, the airport was repaired and expanded. It is now being used for both military and civilian flights. Most of the airport is maintained by the US Armed Forces and the International Security Assistance Force (ISAF), which have large military bases there. The 2009 surge in NATO operations in southern Afghanistan pushed the number of aircraft operations at the base from 1,700 to 5,000 flights a week. The numbers of flights, meant that Kandahar became the busiest one-runway airports in the world. One infamous landmark at Kandahar airport is the aptly name 'poo pond' as quite literally that is what it is full of, poo mixed with wee and cooking oil. The stench from it can be smelt from all corners of the airport, especially with a little bit of wind blowing the wonderful smell. It is a lake of sewage sitting on the intersection of All-American Boulevard and Louisiana Road. It holds the waste produced by 30,000 people using hundreds of portable toilets across the airbase and also holds commercial kitchen grease and cooking oil waste. Rumours are that is has been swam by Special Forces for a bet, but these are unconfirmed rumours. Why anyone in the right mind would want to or even be able to manage to swim across a cesspit is beyond me.

The airport buildings look old and tired. The departure lounge of Kandahar Airbase is a dusty, dirty building with a lounge in name and nothing else. At times it is full of troops and civilians all keen to make their way back home. In total the airbase is home to around 15,000 troops from all over the world and a further 10,000 civilian contractors.

On the tarmac outside, there are military transport planes, fighters and civilian airliners. It is hard to believe it is a military base with the vast swathes of commercial airliners, some contracted to take troops home.

The British contingent at Kandahar consists of around 500 of us, some Army but mainly RAF personnel. It is a truly cosmopolitan society with people from all over the world. A bus driven by an Indian is on hand to ferry everyone around. He will probably do 12 months here before returning home. The bus that was due to ferry me to our accommodation, had a Hamburg, Germany number plate on it. It looked like a slightly old and battered tour bus, how it ended up in Kandahar airport let alone Afghanistan seems to be a complete mystery.

As we started our final short trek, it did not take me long to realise how dusty the environment was. The bus banged and bumped over the pot hole laden road that would take us to our home from home for the next few months. A series of tents greeted us - we were about two miles away from the flight line and our beloved Harriers. It is truly hard to appreciate the size of Kandahar Airbase unless you have been there.

We arrived at our meagre accommodation which looked not too dissimilar to Nissen huts back home creating shared accommodation. It was basic accommodation with shared male and female facilities only the sleeping accommodation was same sex. It was comfortable enough and would be my home for the next few months.

CHAPTER TWO - JTAC

Two A-10s were already on station, but the Hogs had fired everything they had. They were remaining on scene to continue monitoring the situation until we arrived on station. We had raced to the area as soon as we got the call not far from the Pakistani border. One of the Hog pilots 'Griffin' came over the radio to greet us in a broad American accent and give us a quick sitrep short for situation report. The area was swarming with Taliban fighters and the coalition troops were close to being overrun. They had advanced on to a Taliban stronghold and come face to face with 200-250 Taliban fighters. The JTAC on the ground was having a hard time trying to prioritise and direct air support to where it was needed the most. A drone in the form of a Predator was also helping, by lasering targets for laser guided bombs. The area was certainly busy both on the ground and in the air.

Griffin the Warthog driver, told us, "fellas, those guys on the ground need as much support as you can give them, otherwise they will be in a world of pain."

Coalition ground forces were firing back with everything they had, but were outnumbered 5 to 1. If they stopped laying down mortar and small arms fire, even for a second, the Taliban would quickly overrun them. We knew the situation was getting desperate and every second counted. The Predator would lase the target for us.' JTAC was still listing all the other potential targets.

It was like flying into a wasp nest and trying to work out which wasp or group of wasps to attack first. There were Taliban fighters moving in all directions. The crucial part was to identify and neutralize the largest threat. That really was down to a combination of the JTAC and the boots on the ground along with what we could see from the air.

The flight path to ensure there was no accidental collision, required the Harriers to hold on one side of the valley while the Hogs would hold on the other side, because it might be necessary to throw in one of the Hogs for white phosphorus marking, or get some smoke laid down by mortars on the ground for target identification. Our issue was going to be fuel, as this was rapidly being depleted as we undertook tight turns after each run dropping ordnance. The JTAC was screaming more targets than we had fuel, let alone munitions for. The first bombs found their target, but my concern for our fuel levels was becoming greater and greater. We did not have enough fuel to get back to base and would need to find a friendly tanker to refuel.

Fuzz set up to go on another attack run straight away with his final pod of rockets, but the bingo warning was already going off in his ear. He knew that this had to be his last attack as the fuel was now too tight to push it any more. I too went in for my final run of rockets and hit the pickle button, letting of my final salvo on a group of advancing Taliban. We had done all we could and I felt sorry for the JTAC, who could do nothing more than wait for the next asset to arrive on station, and hopefully finish what we started. Tipping the scales in the beleaguered coalition's soldiers' favour.

We quickly climbed up to 29,000 feet and we knew we had to find a friendly tanker to feed our hungry Harriers. Thankfully, there was a tanker only 50 miles away, we would not be too far from vapour but with a bit of economical flying we should make it. After a few tense minutes the KC-135 tanker was in sight, as we drew closer I raised the refuelling probe from the left hand, top side of the engine intakes or elephant ears as they were affectionately called. I began to slow down as I manoeuvred the fuel probe towards the trailing drogue with a fuel line attached. The idea was to get the probe into the basket and maintain a speed about 1 knot faster than the tanker was travelling. It was fairly difficult in the daylight, but almost a nightmare in the pitch black dark. Keeping the Harrier steady was a job in itself as we got buffeted by vortices from the KC-135. Once plugged in, it would take us around 10 minutes to get 5000lb into our tanks, before unplugging and making our way back to Kandahar.

As we got close to Kandahar airbase we began our tactical decent. Looking to the south I could see the beautiful and inhospitable red desert. I put down flaps and gear just as we came into land. I flared the Harrier to slow down and bring it softly onto the shimmering 12,000 foot Kandahar runway. With airbrakes deployed the Harrier soon came to a stop and for an even more rapid stop, we could vector the thrust nozzles fully forward known as a PNB (Power Nozzle Braking). The Harrier has two control elements that a normal fighter does not usually have. The first is the thrust vector created by the four engine nozzles which can be set between 0 degrees and 98 degrees, controlled by a control next to the thrust lever. The second is the reaction controls that behave like the cyclic in a helicopter. These are mainly used at very low speeds and control the pitch and yaw. This reaction control jets are mounted in the wingtips, nose and tail.

All this means, a Harrier pilot needs to be highly skilled. As well as the skills required to fly a fast jet, you need to be able to manually maintain controls to transition from flight to hover and vice versa, where normal flight controls are ineffective. The skills needed for VTOL are more akin to that of a helicopter pilot.

Once at the nearest exit we made our way onto the taxiway and back to our hard standing area, before I opened the canopy to let in the warm dusty air. It is always nice to be back after a combat operation. You do feel different knowing you are in a danger zone, but the beauty of Afghanistan from the air can lead you into a false sense of security.

With our sortie completed it was down to the engineers and maintainers to turn the aircraft around. With the high number of sorties we were currently undertaking it was a huge task keeping all the Harriers flying. They worked 12 hour shifts, 24 hours a day to keep us at 100% availability. Spares were also readily available which also helped maintain availability. Hats off to all of them, for not only the effort they put in, but enduring the severe cold of working through the night or the dust and heat of working through the day. A Harrier could fly 720 hours between a major service. This worked out as 10 months each Harrier could serve in Afghanistan before needing to be sent back to the UK for a major service. Each Harrier had its own personality and you could always tell one that had just arrived from a full service, it felt tight and not quite as responsive for the first few flight hours. ZG477 was no different, you would get used to the quirks and adapt your flying for each Harrier. Some Harriers were a bit like a 'Friday car' always breaking down and having faults appear to test our engineers to their limits.

CHAPTER THREE – HARRIER INCEPTION

To have the versatility of a helicopter and performance of a high speed aircraft, is something designers strived for in the early days of aviation. Various designs were tried and failed. From aircraft that took off vertically powered by large propellers to tilt wings, tilt engines, fans in the wings, augmented engines to name a few. The Harrier was in essence born out of research undertaken with the Rolls Royce developed Thrust Measuring Rig (TMR) also known 'Flying Bedsted.' The Flying Bedstead powered by two Nene turbojets was a pioneering vertical take-off and landing aircraft that first flew in the 1953. The TMR was made up from steel framework with four legs with castors for wheels and used two Nene engines mounted back-to-back horizontally. It proved that stable hovering was possible from a jet engine and paved the way for the Harrier's control system. From the TMR, this led to the Rolls Royce RB108 and the Short SC.1. The SC.1 flew for over ten years, providing a large amount of data that influenced later design concepts such as the "puffer jet" controls on the Hawker Siddeley P.1127, which would later evolve into the Hawker Siddeley Harrier. The US Navy funded the Lockheed XFV-1 and Convair XFY-1 turboprop with tests ceasing in 1956. A third aircraft that took off from its tail, known as a 'tailsitter,' the Ryan X-13 Vertijet, was powered by a Rolls Royce Avon turbojet. The X13 became the world's first jet powered VTOL research aircraft when it flew on 10 December 1955. The Bell X-14 got closer to the Harrier with its vectored thrust engine which first flew in 1957 and went from horizontal to vertical flight on 24 May 1958. However, by 1964 the USAF stuck with the view that V/STOL was not worthwhile and the expectation was the F-111 would sell around the world as a next generation aircraft, effectively holding back V/STOL aircraft development.

The requirement for combat that could be dispersed away from main air bases arose in the early days of the Cold War. As the West fears grew that the Soviet Union would soon possess thousands of nuclear weapons which could potentially wipe out conventional air bases. The big issue with V/STOL aircraft was their cost compared to conventional designs. Another issue was having a powerplant with a much higher than normal thrust to weight ratio.

The key to the Harriers design is the Bristol Pegasus Vectored engine, which would have not existed, but for the Harrier and vice versa. The engine was first proven in the P.1127. Sir Sydney Camm and Bristol's Sir Stanley Hooker got the P.1127 in the air 17 months after cutting the first piece of metal. The design and abilities of the early Harriers were enough to get the interest of the USA and work in partnership with McDonnell Douglas, now Boeing in the design and development of the US built AV8A and AV8B.

The Hawker Siddeley Harrier GR1/GR3 and the AV8A were the first generation of Harrier. They were the first operational close support and reconnaissance attack aircraft with vertical/short takeoff and landing (V/STOL) capabilities. These were developed directly from the Hawker P.1127 prototype and the Kestrel evaluation aircraft. Kestrel development began in 1957, taking advantage of the Bristol Engine Company's choice to invest in the creation of the Pegasus vectored-thrust engine. Testing began in July 1960 and by the end of the year the aircraft had achieved both vertical take-off and horizontal flight. The test program also explored the possibility of use upon aircraft carriers, landing on HMS Ark Royal in 1963. The first three aircraft crashed during testing, one at the 1963 Paris Air Show. The RAF went on to order the Harrier GR1 and GR3 variants in the late 1960s. The Harrier GR.1 made its first flight on 28 December 1967. Officially entered service with the RAF on 18 April 1969. The GR3 was an upgrade to the GR1 with improved sensors, a nose-mounted laser tracker, the integration of ECM systems and a further upgraded Pegasus 11 or Mk 103 with 21,000 lbf up from the original 19,000 lbf of thrust on the first GR1s. Which was quite a leap from the P.1127 prototype which had only 13,500 lbf of thrust.

The Sea Harrier was the naval version of the Hawker Siddeley Harrier. It was designed as a V/STOL jet fighter, reconnaissance and attack aircraft. The first version entered service with the Royal Navy's Fleet Air Arm in April 1980 as the Sea Harrier FRS1, and was informally known as the Shar. The upgraded Sea Harrier FA2 entered service in 1993. It was withdrawn from Royal Navy service in March 2006, when the cost of upgrading it to the GR9 standard was too costly. The Royal Navy gained use of the GR7/GR9 until the Harriers retirement. The Sea Harrier FRS Mk51 is still in active service with the Indian Navy, which operates the jet from its aircraft carrier INS Viraat.

The Harrier II which followed the US AV8A and RAF GR3 was extensively redeveloped by McDonnell Douglas and British Aerospace leading to the Boeing/BAE Systems AV8B Harrier II. This second-generation V/STOL jet multi-role aircraft, including the British Aerospace-built Harrier GR5/GR7/GR9, which entered service in the mid-1980s. The AV8B is primarily used for light attack or multi-role tasks, typically operated from small aircraft carriers. Versions are used by several NATO countries, including Spain, Italy, and the United States. The Harrier II was an extensively modified version of the first generation Harrier. The original aluminium alloy fuselage was replaced by a fuselage which made extensive use of composites, providing significant weight reduction and increased payload or range. A new one-piece wing provided around 14 per cent more area and increased thickness. The wing and leading-edge root extensions allowed for a 6,700-pound payload increase over a 1,000 ft takeoff compared with the first generation Harriers. The Harrier IIs also had an additional missile pylon in front of each wing landing gear, and strengthened leading edges of the wings to meet higher bird strike requirements. Avionics were upgraded and a bubble canopy added to improve visibility along with a hands-on-throttle-and-stick system (HOTAS) to help make the Harrier II easier to fly. Between 1969 and 2003, 824 Harrier variants were delivered. While the manufacture of new Harriers finished in 1997, the last re-manufactured aircraft a Harrier II Plus configuration, was delivered in December 2003 which ended the Harrier production line. The Harrier II has participated in numerous conflicts, making significant contributions in combat theatres such as Kosovo, Iraq, and Afghanistan. The Harrier's main function was as a platform for air interdiction and close air support missions; the Harrier II was also used for reconnaissance duties until its retirement in 2010.

The GR9 version was the final multi-role combat version that could operate at night and at low-light levels in extreme environments, from a wide selection of locations including aircraft carriers and forward air bases. The GR9 was equipped with night-vision goggles and forward-looking infrared (FLIR). The GR9s new navigation system was able to provide highly accurate navigation. The system also included a ring laser gyroscope inertial navigation system which was coupled to a GPS system.

The Harrier GR9 was armed with general-purpose bombs and cluster munitions, Paveway laser and GPS guided bombs against buildings. The Raytheon AGM-65 Maverick infrared guided anti-tank missiles and AIM-9 Sidewinder short-range air-to-air missile. The AIM-9 was originally developed by the United States Navy in the 1950s.

The Raytheon Paveway IV precision guided bomb were at the time, the latest generation of the Paveway family and entered service on the Harrier GR9 aircraft deployed to Afghanistan in December 2008. The Paveway IV used both laser guidance and GPS-aided inertial navigation. The Paveway IV incorporated anti-spoofing and anti-jamming technology. The weapon has good manoeuvrability and following launch it can even turn around and attack a target behind the aircraft delivering it. The GPS/IN system is supplied by Raytheon Systems at Glenrothes, Scotland. In order to attack relocatable and moving targets or fixed targets, the pilot was able to switch between guidance modes as necessary before or after weapon release. Paveway IV was fitted with enhanced mk82 500lb warheads designed by Raytheon Missile Systems in Tucson. EDO MBM Technology based in Brighton was responsible for the supply of the Paveway IV aircraft umbilical interconnect system and quad containers. The Raytheon

AGM-65 Maverick is a man-in-the-loop, low collateral damage, anti-tank and anti-ship, close air support missile.

The Brimstone anti-armour system was deployed on the GR9 from 2008. The MBDA UK Brimstone fire-and-forget missile has a millimetre wave seeker operating at 94GHz which provides all-weather day-and-night capability. The missile is armed with a tandem high-explosive warhead. The Harrier GR9 is not fitted with a gun but can be armed with CRV7 rockets in pods on under wing hardpoints.

One of the main roles of the Harrier though, was close air support which involved launching air attacks against hostile targets in close proximity to friendly forces. Harriers are usually employed in direct support of ground troops operating against enemy troop positions, tanks and artillery. Harriers were also used for the air interdiction role in which the aircraft carry out low or medium-level attacks using precision-guided, free fall or retarded bombs. The Harrier GR.9 was also deployed on strike coordination and reconnaissance (SCAR) operations. Harriers were withdrawn from the Afghan theatre in June 2009, they were subsequently replaced by several RAF Tornado GR4s.

CHAPTER FOUR – INSURGENT HUNT

A 0600 wake up call, I dragged myself out of bed and into the cold morning air. After a quick breakfast, I made my way to the ops rooms for a briefing, before going on standby and awaiting the call to scramble. We did not have to wait long before a call came through. We jumped into a Land Cruiser and made our way quickly to the flight line. ZG477 had the early morning sun glinting off the canopy as we drew up to the flight line. After a quick check round the outside and a chat for any issues, I climbed into the cockpit, got strapped in with the help of ground crew and began pre-flight checks. The Pegasus engine burst into life and we were soon on our way along the taxiway towards the end of the runway at Kandahar. The GR9 Harriers were originally fitted with the Pegasus MK105 engine providing 21,750lb and the GR9A Harriers fitted with the higher rated Pegasus MK107 engine providing 23,400lb thrust. The GR9A with the higher rated engine was also modified to incorporate a new metal, high-fatigue rated, rear fuselage section as well.

We were given immediate takeoff clearance. As soon as I had turned onto the runway and was straight, I pushed the throttle fully forward, holding the brakes on before releasing them, moments later. The noise of the Pegasus engine rose to a high pitch scream as the Harrier leapt forward, pushing me back into the seat. On takeoff, you always needed to concentrate on keeping the aircraft flying straight as it rocked slightly from side to side as it gathered speed. With a final glance at my instruments to check everything was fine, I pulled back on the stick and ZG477 leapt into the air. I quickly got the gear up and heard the reassuring thud telling me the gear was locked. I kept the climb very shallow, allowing ZG477 to pick up speed, reducing my flaps before going into a steeper climb. As I pulled back harder I could feel the g increase and the air pressure drop as I climbed higher in a tactical departure. As I climbed I was alternating my attention between the Harrier's instrumentation – particularly the engine-monitoring systems – and the mirrors. Even though no coalition aircraft had ever been shot down on departure from Kandahar Airfield, I still stayed vigilant watching for any tell-tale signs of a SAM on my six. As soon as I got above 20,000, there was some relief. My wingman, Fuzz formed up on my wing and we followed our vector to our targets. As we travelled, we both checked all our weapon systems were working and uncaged the targeting pod. I checked the pod by getting it to lock onto a waypoint I had just selected. This meant everything was working and the pod and aircraft talking to each other properly.

After we had done the mutual, laser, flare and radio check. I ran through my own checklist - reaching down to the distinctive brown and white pattern of the Late Arm switch on the left-hand side of the cockpit, and switched it to live. Some Harrier pilots have a different preference, but I like to have my Late Arm on all the time when airborne. It stops me forgetting to have to arm each time I select a weapon. With a final visual check outside, I knew ZG477 was ready for battle. I had the usual complement of 540lb bombs, CRV-7 rockets and a couple of 1,000lb Paveway laser guided bombs.

We headed towards Helmand province at 450 knots, Royal Marines were a man down after an IED (Improvised Explosive Device) strike. The Royal Marines had been heading back after a successful patrol and only two miles from their FOB (Forward Operating Base). The problem with Helmand was the number of choke points caused by the elaborate network of canals.

Afghanistan has 34 provinces, of which, Helmand is the largest. It is named after the Helmand River that begins in the Hindu Kush mountain range, which is to the west of Kabul. The Helmand River flows for 1000 miles before finally evaporating into the marshes at the Iranian border. The Helmand basin has long been a trading route between Persia and India. It is the same route that has been used by many armies for thousands of years. The capital of Helmand Province is Lashkar Bazzar, which translates into English as 'Army Barracks'. The canals and waterways that were so dangerous to navigate, especially for troops on the ground, had been rebuilt from the old network of canals along the Helmand River, and new ones added. In the 1930s, the Germans and

Japanese reconnected 9 miles of a 200-year-old stretch, just before the outbreak of the Second World War. After the Second World War the Americans came along with the Helmand Valley Project in 1946. The project was designed to irrigate 300,000 acres of desert to the west and north of Lashkar Gah, and then settle 20,000 nomadic tribe people. The project lasted until 1979 and cost $136.5 million. All Americans left in August 1979, just before the Soviet invasion. The Helmand Valley Project became an expensive failure, leaving a complex tribal system in place that was quite fragile and somewhat volatile.

As we got on scene we could see the choke point that had made it so easy for the Taliban to plant an IED and then ambush the Royal Marines. The canals had steep sides, which offered protection, but also limited visibility. The vehicles had no choice but to travel on the surface, although most vehicles offered some protection, apart from IEDs, which could rip a more lightly armoured vehicles like a Humvee in half, even those with greater armour like a Mastif could lose a wheel from an IED blast.

The Taliban had decided to position an IED on a popular convoy route. It was a regular tactic employed by the insurgents. If they could identify a route that was in frequent use by coalition troops, they would conceal some form of IED the most popular being a pressure-plate IED, buried under the vehicle tracks or sometimes just beside them. A canal crossing was a prime location for an

IED. The only way to find them was to have a soldier up front doing a 'Barma,' basically using a Vallon, a form of metal detector to look for hidden IEDs. From the air the blast site of the IED could clearly be seen; down the side of the canal a group of Royal Marines working on their fallen comrade. A wrecked front cab section of BVS10 Viking tracked vehicle could clearly be seen and the driver was most likely the one now being tended o by his comrades. The Viking is a twin cab design with each cab section having its own set of tracks. Their low ground pressure is not enough to trigger most of the anti-tank mines in use in Afghanistan, but they have proved vulnerable to IEDs, as they do not have a v-shaped hull or substantial under body armour.

A Chinook medevac helicopter was on its way out to pick up the wounded Marine and take him to the medical centre at Camp Bastion, but until that happened the patrol had no option but to stay in its present position. The location was far from ideal as offered limited cover and protection and the Taliban had already started their ambush. I could hear the stress in the JTACs voice as he vectored me into their position. He required me to perform a recce and get eyes on the Taliban as he was unable to do so from his current position.

The moment the device had detonated, the patrol had dismounted and spread out into all round defence as quickly as they could, but they were right in the middle of a classic Taliban ambush and for the moment they were pinned down. They were basically penned in by Taliban forces and the heavily damaged Viking was also blocking their egress route.

Every Marine in the patrol knew that there could be hundreds of heavily armed Taliban fighters, travelling to the area to reinforce the Taliban. The Marines were expecting at any moment to come under fire from heavy machine guns and RPGs. The Marines did have some heavier weapons and mortars along with their personal issue SA80 A2.

"Six Four, Six Four. Stay at twenty and watch the outer perimeter. I'll go down and check out the rest." I throttled back and pointed the nose of the Harrier towards the ground. The first thing we had to do was to eliminate any blind spots – not difficult from the air – and then expand the safe perimeter around the troops. Dropping down to about 3,000 feet, I began to fly a circle around the main canal crossing point. I trimmed the aircraft so that I could almost fly it with only the smallest amount of input from me. I put on the altitude hold and started checking the area below me. I made use of the gyro-stabilized binoculars in the Harrier's cockpit. These were easy to use and allowed me to survey a considerable area very quickly. They would help me make a better tactical picture and decide which targets to take out first. Once I had located a possible target, I then made use of the Harrier's targeting pod, a very high-fidelity sensor, to examine the location through the optics on the flat screen in the cockpit, and to refine the coordinates. The equipment wasn't actually designed for this task, although Harrier pilots had achieved considerable success with it. There's no denying that the sensors are highly sophisticated pieces of equipment, but for optimum and efficient use the pilot must first locate the target, or at least its rough position. The next task is to move the sensor on to the position. Using the wrecked Viking as my reference point, I began a visual search of the immediate area and the surrounding area. I remained in constant radio contact with the JTAC on the ground, updating them of positions so they could also get a more accurate picture of the unfolding battle and pass it on to the boots on the ground.

Rather than look for individual or groups of Insurgents I tried to look at potential firing points and routes in and out of the immediate area. I was able to identify some firing points as well as groups of Taliban. Some, however, were a best guess of where I thought they may be able to conceal themselves. I took ZG477 down to a 1000 feet for my final circuit with my wingman acting as a spotter for any RPGs or worse still SAMs being fired in our direction.

After the final circuit, we had identified several primary targets and even more secondary targets. I put ZG477 into a tight turn once again feeling the g push me down into my seat and the bladders on my g suit 'speed jeans' inflate around my legs. I pointed the nose of ZG477 at a large mound surrounded by vegetation and hit the pickle button. Several CRV7 70mm folding fin rockets raced away at Mach 5 before their 4.5Kg warhead found the target and a wall of flame and dust rose into the sky. One target down, we then systematically worked our way through each target until all our rockets had been expended. We did have the Paveway and 540lb airburst bomb. The problem was the vicinity of civilian buildings and also the Royal Marines. An Apache helicopter was on its way to bring in the next wave of air support and we decided to climb higher and circle, passing on enemy positions for the Apache to make use of and allow not only the Chinook Medvac helicopter to get in and land - but at the same time allow the Royal Marines to make a tactical retreat out of the area as well.

CHAPTER FIVE – PEGASUS ENGINE

The Bristol and later Rolls Royce Pegasus engine story, is one that started in the late 1940s, immediately following World War II. The development of ballistic missiles and sophisticated munitions led to concern in the Western Alliance regarding the vulnerability of North Atlantic Treaty Organization (NATO) airfields.

The two UK companies to become responsible for Pegasus and Harrier development were, at this time, not active in the field of VTO. The Bristol Aeroplane Company Engine Division, later to be absorbed into Bristol Siddeley Engines and then into Rolls-Royce, had responded to a requirement for a light-weight engine to power a NATO strike fighter, conventional in configuration but able to operate from relatively unprepared runways. This engine, the Orpheus turbojet, was selected for the Fiat G91 aircraft to meet the NATO requirement. The development program was managed and funded by the Mutual Weapons Development Program (MWDP), a United States agency with an office in Paris having the objective of supporting projects of potential value to the NATO forces. The Fiat G91, which later entered service with the German and Italian air forces, was to be followed in a second-phase program by an aircraft with enhanced performance and in a third phase by a strike fighter with short take-off and vertical-landing capability.

In March 1956, when MWDP was turning its attention to the third phase, NATO requirement, a proposal was submitted to the Paris office by Michel Wibault. Wibault was well known in aviation in the pre-war period, the company of that name having been responsible for a range of French transport and fighter aircraft. Post-war Wibault had been working on novel aviation projects and had produced schemes for a VSTOL strike fighter, which were entitled "Ground Attack Gyropter," the subject of the March proposal.

This proposal introduced the concept of thrust vectoring and described the basic principles of operation that were subsequently incorporated into the Pegasus engine and the Harrier airframe. The system proposed consisted of a turboprop engine, the Bristol BE25 Orion of about 8,000 horsepower, driving four large centrifugal compressors, arranged like wheels at the sides of the fuselage. The blower casings could be rotated to direct the compressed air, and hence the thrust, through over 90 degrees. The air was directed downwards for vertical takeoff and landing, obliquely for climbing or transition, and horizontally for level flight. The exhaust gas from the turboprop was also used for vertical or horizontal thrust using a gas deviator mechanically connected with the rotation of the four blower casings. The proposed aircraft was stabilized in hovering and low-speed flight by means of air bleed from the compressors and ejected from the wing tips and nose and tail of the airframe.

Col. John Driscoll, at the time head of the MWDP Paris office, sent the proposal to Dr. Stanley Hooker (later Sir Stanley) at Bristol Engines. It was studied by Gordon Lewis, who was responsible for new projects. Lewis recognized the importance of the thrust vectoring principle, but considered the Wibault mechanical arrangement of four compressors driven by shafts and bevel gear boxes to be complex and heavy. He proposed an alternative lighter and simpler arrangement, substituting a two-stage axial flow fan for the four centrifugal.

Wibault Gyropter scheme using BE 48 blowers and vectoring the thrust through two rotating nozzles, one on each side of the engine. This layout, designated BE 48, retained the Orion engine and a reduction gear to drive the fan Further weight reduction resulted from using a power turbine running at the appropriate speed, dispensing with the reduction gear, and replacing the turboprop with the simpler and lighter Orpheus turbojet. The resulting design, the BE 52, was further evolved into the BE 53 with a three-stage fan.

Wibault quickly accepted the changes to his mechanical design and produced a scheme of a strike fighter using the new proposed engine. This was presented to MWDP, where Col. Willis Chapman, later Brigadier General, had replaced Col. Driscoll.

Chapman encouraged Bristol to proceed with the design, and a joint patent was registered at the end of 1956 in the names of Wibault and Lewis. This patent identified the main feature of rotating nozzles, including a pair at the rear of the aircraft to deflect the turbine exhaust gas, and contra-rotation of the engine spools to minimize the effect of gyroscopic couples on hovering stability. By this time the benefit of using a proportion of the fan delivery air to supercharge the engine compressor had been realized, resulting in the necessity for only a single air intake. This aspect was covered in the patent, and the engine emerged as a turbofan, or bypass engine, an arrangement used extensively in later commercial engines.

In May 1957 Sir Sydney Camm of Hawker Aircraft contacted Sir Stanley Hooker to dis-cuss possible VSTOL projects. The BE 53 schemes were presented, and Ralph Hooper of Hawkers carried out a series of project designs aiming at a VSTOL fighter with real military capability. His work contributed much to the refinement of the engine design, including the major feature of rotating rear nozzles, exiting on each side of the fuselage and closely integrated with the engine. The nozzle rotation mechanism had received much attention by F. C. Marchant, in charge of the Bristol design office, and he evolved the scheme of using large diameter bearings to support the nozzles with air motor driven chains round the periphery of the bearings to effect rotation.

By the autumn of 1957, the Hawker designers had prepared the initial schemes of the prototype P.1127, and the engine design, named Pegasus, had become a compact and light thrust vectoring engine, with the thrust line passing through the centre of gravity in all angles of deflection. The engine configuration at the commencement of joint MWDP and company-funded development in 1958 comprised a two-stage fan, seven-stage compressor, and three stages of turbine.

The program moved forward rapidly when Hawker launched the P.1127 prototype with UK funding, and in September 1959, the first engine ran on the test bed, giving 9,000 lbs of thrust. The Hawker Chief Test Pilot, Bill Bedford, flew the P.1127 for the first time in the hovering mode in October 1960, by which time the engine thrust had been increased to 12,000 lbs. John Dale, who had been responsible for development of the Orpheus engine in the Fiat G91, took charge of Pegasus development engineering and led the team that over the years progressively raised the engine thrust to over 23,000 lbs for the RAF' GR9A Harriers and US Marine Corps AV-8Bs.

The Pegasus Harrier combination has been very successful, but nevertheless there have been design and development problems to be solved during its career. The Pegasus early problems emerged.

Intake ducting and fan outlet system. Because the engine has to be located at the aircraft. Early Hawker P.1127 configuration centre of gravity, the intake duct is only about one diameter long. Connecting the two large fuselage side intakes with the engine face required short high curvature ducting, which introduced air flow distortion at the fan inlet and led to excessive blade vibration. To keep the vibration frequencies of the blades outside the revolutions-per-minute (RPM) range of the engine, they were machined with interblade supports and made in titanium for added strength. This also solved the problem of further air distortion caused by the fan outlet ducting. The early faired ducts to the nozzles were replaced by a plenum chamber to insulate the fan from the upstream effect of the two nozzles.

Exhaust duct: The task of the exhaust duct is similar to that of the plenum chamber, that is, to split the flow of gas from the turbine into two nozzles. This induced vibration in the final-stage turbine blades, and the development engineers introduced wire lacing as used in steam turbines to restrain the blade movements. Later in the program, the turbine was redesigned with shrouded blades, also similar to steam turbine practice. With nozzles down, the jets impinge on the ground and can cause erosion of the surface and throw up debris with damaging effects.

The technique of rolling takeoff, making use of the thrust vectoring principle, enabled this issue to be brought under control by accelerating the aircraft forward before directing the nozzles downward. Hot gas recirculation. During jet-borne flight close to the ground, the exhaust gases recirculate round the aircraft and can enter the engine intake and produce temperature rise and flow distortion effects, which reduce engine power. These effects are caused mainly by "fountains" of exhaust gas that form between pairs of jet streams.

The Pegasus, with four nozzles, produces two fountains, the one nearest the intake comprising relatively cool air from the fan, which effectively forms a barrier preventing hot exhaust gas from reaching the intake. Problems of this nature are intrinsically associated with a VTO system, and the Pegasus configuration was demonstrated to have particular advantages over most alternatives. The engine and airframe companies worked closely together throughout the program to solve such problems associated with engine installation. This close collaboration was a special feature of the Pegasus Harrier program.

CHAPTER SIX – HELMAND HORROR

The bases that the U.S. Marines occupied were made deliberately spartan so that US Marines would feel happiest out on patrol, living out of their rucksacks. At one such FOB, which the Marines were sharing with the Afghan Army, the latrines were a disgusting mixture of flies and human excrement that in 40 degree heat led to an unbearable stench. The smell was so bad in the latrines that some soldiers actually wore a gas mask to use them.

In Helmand Province alone, there were now some 20,000 US Marines alongside 9500 British troops. The Marines had both the resources and the manpower to do what the British Army was struggling to do in Helmand. The manpower and equipment needed was quite vast and Helmand was one of the toughest areas with the most amount of Taliban contacts. Most of this was due to the fertile land in Helmand being ideal for growing poppies. Helmand is often referred to as the 'Green Zone' due to the amount of lush green vegetation in the area supplied by water from the Helmand River and the various irrigation ditches and canals. From the air, they looked like a green patchwork quilt.

Our Harriers were to be part of a big push in Helmand, supporting the coalition troops against various targets along with disrupting and destroying the opium supply and production in the area. Opium is an opioid or narcotic made from the white liquid in the poppy plant. Opium contains approximately 12% morphine, an alkaloid, which is frequently processed, chemically for the illegal drug trade in order to produce heroin. The latex in the poppy also includes codeine and non-narcotic alkaloids such as thebaine, papaverine and noscapine. The actual production of opium has changed very little over thousands of years.

Opium production begins with the skin of the ripening pods of poppies being scored by a sharp blade at a time carefully chosen so that rain, wind, and dew cannot spoil the exudation of the white, milky latex substance contained within the pod. It is usually done in the afternoon, and then the milk white substance called 'poppy tears' is allowed to dry overnight into a sticky brown resin to be collected the following morning.

One acre harvested in this way can produce three to five kilograms of raw opium. Crude laboratories close to poppy fields are capable of refining opium into a morphine base via a simple acid-base extraction. This produces a sticky, brown paste, which is pressed into bricks and sun-dried. These almost black-looking bricks, when dried, can be smoked, prepared into other forms or processed into heroin.

Today, the Marines were going in to dismantle a large opium production facility run by the Taliban. The Taliban offered decent rates of pay to entice the locals to come and work for them. The rates of pay were much higher than they would get elsewhere and enough to entice many to work for the Taliban. The farmers also benefited financially by growing poppies, as they too got paid much more for growing poppies than other crops. The soils in Helmand, being moist and alkaline, were ideal for growing poppies and explained why there were so many poppy fields in Helmand. Fields for poppy cultivation in Helmand quadrupled between 2005 and 2008 to 103,590 hectares. To try and stop farmers growing poppies, the United States, Denmark and Britain has financed a $13 million-a-year programme to distribute subsidised wheat and fertiliser to 42,000 Helmand farmers. The farmers end up paying only a quarter of the market price of the package, making it much more profitable than poppies.

The Marines had been tasked with attacking a production facility. Being a production facility and the product and money involved in terms of raw opium. It was reported to be heavily guarded by at least thirty Taliban fighters equipped with AK47s, PK, RPG and a couple of DsHKs. Due to its locality, it was also difficult to get tanks in to offer fire support, so we were assigned to go in instead. It had been a lucky tasking, as it should have gone to the F15s, but a technical issue and maintenance meant the USAF was short of aircraft to cover the mission. The USAF or US Marines tended to get the best missions, partly due to availability of planes and munitions, but also the Americans obsession with ensuring its ground forces always got the best close air support possible.

The main issue with this mission was ensuring that none of the locals were injured in the raid, as this would cause propaganda issues. It was imperative I ensured I hit the targets and selected the correct weapons. I walked out with my wingman Fuzz to our awaiting GR.9s, fully armed with a selection of PRV7 rockets and 540lb airburst bombs. XG477 looking suave in its air defence grey paint, that actually replaced their western European dark-green camouflage in 1993. Air defence grey was judged to be more effective at higher altitudes.

I gave the usual walk around and ensured the data black box had been inserted with all the mission data pre-loaded onto it. I then checked the undercarriage, ordnance, flaps and general condition before climbing up the ladder to the cockpit, where a member of the ground crew ensured I was strapped in properly.

"Ready to go, sir?" asked the ground crew member.

"Yes," I replied, as I flicked the various switches before starting the Pegasus engine and waiting for it to get up to operating speed. Minutes later, I was told by air traffic control I could take off. I could already feel the heat in the cockpit. Being a desert climate the temperatures could be quite extreme from -2 in the early morning to over 30 degrees by early afternoon. The Harrier had sat under the tent like hide structure away from the morning sunshine. As I taxied out onto the taxiway the heat started to seep into the cockpit and I could feel sweat trickling down his face.

The cockpit would cool down soon enough as I roared down the runway at full throttle before lifting off for a tactical ascent to patrol altitude. It was a 20 minute flight to our objective, passing over a patchwork of green fields at 20,000 feet before dropping down to 200 feet as we got close to our objective.

Over a hundred US Marines were involved in the operation, which, along with the main production facility was to further disrupt the supply of opium by destroying any supply convoys or vehicles suspected of carrying narcotics. The surrounding poppy fields were also to be destroyed with the aid of the Afghan Army.

The U.S. Marines Corp was originally formed in 1775, their mission has changed and evolved and they have been involved in every American war and conflict since 1775. In November 2001, the 15th and 26th Marine Expeditionary Units were the first conventional forces into Afghanistan in support of Operation Enduring. The Marines then went on to seize Kandahar International Airport in December 2001, with the help of the British SBS.

By the time I had got halfway to the objective, the US Marines had already been targeted and were coming under quite intense fire. They had got themselves trapped in a compound that had a small perimeter wall around it which was ideal for setting up fire support in the form of an M249 light machine gun (LMG). The downside was that they were unable to move forward due to enemy fire coming from multiple arcs. The roof of the compound had ten Marines stationed on it - one with a 60mm mortar that had already begun to lay down effective fire on the Taliban fighters.

The Taliban's rate of fire was quite immense for a position that was only said to have about 30 insurgents. To the Marines, it felt like there were much more than 30. Rounds were ricocheting off the compound walls, leaving a small puff of smoke and an indentation as each round hit. A strong smell of cordite filled the air as the US Marines started to lay down fire. One Marine had already been shot in the shoulder. It had been a through-and-through, though. Meaning that the bullet had gone right through him and into the wall behind. He was dragged back into the compound for the medic to start treating him. He would require a medevac, but at the moment there was no chance of that, such was the intensity of the ensuing fire fight.

I knew we needed to get a move on and pushed the throttles forward to pick up the pace slightly and get on station sooner. As we approached, JTAC gave the coordinates for the location of the various enemy positions which were forward of the opium production facility and away from any potential civilians working there. To reduce any potential civilian casualties I did a low and fast pass just to get a visual on civilian positions. Luckily they were all close to the facility with enough distance from the Taliban positions for on target rockets to do the business.

The first pass Rockets kicked up a large amount of dust and smoke in a long line in front of the compound from which the US Marines were firing. This restricted the view for both the US Marines and the Taliban. With one pass completed and half the Taliban fighters lying dead, the order was given for the US Marines huddled down by the front wall of the compound to move forward, whilst those on the roof would give fire support. We would give a further pass and drop a 540lb airburst bomb on a larger Taliban position that was still firing despite being hit by rockets. I banked my Harrier into a steep turn, feeling the high g, as I did. I relayed back various ground targets after I dropped my 540lb bomb. To help direct the US Marines to any final positions as they made their advance. With a jet overhead, some of the Taliban were now redirecting their fire at my Harrier, further giving relief to the US Marines on the attack. 60mm mortar fire was still raining down on some Taliban fighters, still dug in at a treeline just to the right of the production facility. JTAC then requested that my wingman go in and destroy the position with 540lb airburst bomb, that landed on target with a bright orange and yellow flash that sent a plume of dirt and debris into the sky. The bomb had found its target and obliterated the enemy position, destroying several trees in the process and enabling the

US Marines to move further to the objective without any further loss of life or injury. As I circled back around, I noticed two Taliban fighters moving up towards the US Marines and I was able to fire my last rockets, killi the Taliban fighters in the process.

The US Marines now had the upper hand and were easily able to take out the remaining Taliban fighters and storm the production facility to capture the objective. Along with the objective, they managed to capture several prisoners who could be useful for intelligence purposes. With fuel running low and 'bingo' fuel alarms sounding it was time to join up with a tanker and take on board some fuel mid-air before returning back to base. You could set your own 'bingo' – low-level – fuel at a higher figure than the minimum, which I did all the time, because when you reached that state you could then decide whether to stay on station or go. The Harrier has its own sets of warnings for when the fuel level gets really low. These warnings will come on and stay on. The warning appears in two stages: steady and then flashing when fuel is critically low. When both lights come on steadily, it means you're down to about 750lb each side, which is enough for about 100 miles of flight. Double flashing bingo lights mean 250lb on either side. With 500lb of fuel remaining you have around eight minutes of flight left at the most economical burn and only three minutes at full throttle. The Harrier's biggest drawback was always its range even with drop tanks.

CHAPTER SEVEN – SPECIAL BOAT SERVICE

Soltani, Regional Command East, had requested fire support, with my wingman Fuzz, we were scrambled and immediately raced out to our awaiting Harriers, before quickly getting strapped in, undertaking quick pre-flight checks and setting off. We had been called to go and support some Special Forces who were under heavy attack on the Pakistani border. The SBS had gone in, to capture a local Taliban commander and had hit resistance that had ended up higher than expected. The position had a greater number of Taliban than expected and heavier weapons than expected too.

We raced to the scene, knowing that every second counted for the guys on the ground. Being in the air was generally far, far safer than being on the ground under intense fire. The odd stray bullet may come our way, a SAM was our only real threat along with effective AA fire. There was quite low cloud cover today, with the base at 4000 feet and the tops varied between 11,000 and 26,000 feet. This hindered visibility a little, but once on station, I could see the fierce fire fight below. The SBS had become virtually pinned down by the sheer volume of fire along with the weight of Taliban fighters. I knew we needed to even the odds and give the Special Forces a chance.

Due to the close proximity of the Taliban to the SBS, we could only use our rockets carefully and would strafe the Taliban from behind the SBS. My first pass concentrated on the main group of Taliban laying down fire; from just behind a wall, just outside the main compound. I aimed for the wall itself, hoping that would catch the Taliban fighters crouched behind it and firing over the top. As I approached the target I could see the muzzle flashes coming from the various positions. I lined up via my HUD and hit the pickle button.

The rockets ripped through both the Taliban and the wall, like a knife through butter, tearing many of the Taliban apart in a large cloud of dust. Many, though, upon hearing an attacking jet, had taken cover where they could find it, and they popped back out after I had made my first pass.

Pushing ZG477 into a tight turn and 45 degree bank, I went back around for another pass, while my wingman flew in and fired rockets at another Taliban position. With a single pass he had killed seven Taliban fighters instantaneously as his rockets rained down on them. The SBS was now getting some room to breathe - rather than just laying down covering fire, this meant they could start to move up, onto their objective. We went in with several more passes, meaning the assault by the SBS could pick up the pace and become dynamic once again. Sadly, they also had a casualty with a serious bullet wound to his leg; whilst still alive, he would not be for much longer if they did not get him any proper medical attention ASAP. The SBS operative had been lucky as it had just missed his femoral artery by millimetres.

In anger, some of the Taliban fighters were aiming us. We were getting a couple of non-vital hits on both our airframes. Some more holes for the ground crew to patch up on our return and moan about how badly we treated their pride and joy.

We had let off a couple of salvos of rockets and this had helped the SBS, get right up on their target with greatly reduced fire from the Taliban. The SBS had a local Taliban commander to take captive if they could, and the Taliban was going to ensure this was no easy task. The Taliban was fighting with much more vigour and showing much greater resistance. Even with air support overhead, the Taliban had no intention of fleeing this time.

We get overhead recording the attack and keeping a watchful eye for any Taliban forces coming in to reinforce. As the true professionals that the SBS are, I was simply in awe as they went in after a fierce firefight got their man, and got out. I have bumped into these guys, several times before, they are often overshadowed by the SAS, but they are more than up to the task and a great bunch of blokes.

With the SBS out and quickly get some distance between them and the Taliban. We watched their egress and put down a couple of rockets on the compound to try to cut off any pursing Taliban. Normally, with air support on scene, the Taliban would start to flee rather than risk being killed after a few passes. But with the SBS having captured a local commander who the Taliban did not want to fall into enemy hands, they fought back ferociously. Taliban fighters were still hot on the SBSs tail.

We went in for a couple more strafing runs with rockets; the Taliban fighters started to pull back and retreat. We had managed to halt the pursuers and give the SBS even greater breathing room to disappear into the night. The final part of our op, was to provide top cover for the UH60 Black Hawk on its final leg to pick up the SBS and their prisoner. In a matter of minutes the Black Hawk was on the deck picking up the SBS and off into the night flying low and fast - with us flying top cover for the first part of the Black Hawks flight.

With fuel low and an uneventful flight back to Kandahar, Fuzz touched down first and opened up his airbrakes, before reversing the thrusters using PNB, before coming to an abrupt stop. I followed suit and within minutes we were back on the hard standing. The ground crew swarmed around us to begin refuelling and rearming both or Harrier ready for the next call to scramble. It gave me a chance to go to the ops room and grab a coffee and a couple of chocolate biscuits to give me a sugar boost as I waited for the next call to come in. I don't mind night shifts as long as I am busy. The adrenaline from each scramble keeps you awake and by being busy, you also forget that you are tired. The worst part is between 4 and 5am, when your body is screaming out for you to sleep. We would scramble a further two times before dawn broke. Then it was finally time to get our heads down before a couple of days off from ops.

CHAPTER EIGHT – CAMP BASTIAN

So far during the war in Afghanistan, there have been 159 aircraft losses - 121 rotary wing and 38 fixed wing. Of these, only 38 have been due to hostile fire. As for UK Harriers, one has been damaged and two have been written off. On 14 October 2005, a

GR7A was destroyed and another damaged in a rocket attack by Taliban forces while parked on the tarmac at Kandahar. No one was injured in the attack. The damaged Harrier was repaired at the airfield while the destroyed one was replaced by another fighter which flew out from Britain on the same evening. On 14 May 2009, after an uneventful sortie to Harrier GR9s returned to Kandahar airport. However, they were held off by ten minutes due to aircraft waiting to land and depart. When cleared to land ATC requested an expedite landing and runway clearance due to heavy traffic as both aircraft were getting very close to bingo fuel.

The wingman landed first due to low fuel. In doing so he received a hostile missile alert and released flares. ZG478's turn onto finals was too short and 6,500ft higher than normal. Throughout the approach the rate of descent was too high and 'Hover Stop' was selected in an attempt to correct this. At 180ft full power was selected, but the tail struck the ground 30ft from the threshold. The outriggers and main undercarriage collapsed as did the nose wheel when the aircraft pitched forward. The under wing stores (bombs, rockets, recce pod, targeting pod and drop tanks) caught fire as the aircraft slid along the runway for 4,000ft. During the slide the pilot turned the aircraft away from a formation of four aircraft waiting to take off, then ejected when it came to a stand. The fire spread to engulf the whole aircraft, causing a total loss and the aircraft ZG478 was subsequently written off.

The biggest single loss of Harriers was undertaken by 19 Taliban fighters dressed in United States Army uniforms. They destroyed six and badly damaged to AV8B Harriers of the US Marines during an attack on Camp Bastion in Afghanistan.

Camp Bastion is four miles long by two miles wide - built by 39 Royal Engineers. The British decided to call the new camp Bastion – a reference to the huge earth-filled bags that have been used to define its boundaries. The bomb-proof bags are made by a UK company called Hesco Bastion, which was set up by a British inventor, Jimi Heselden. He has made a small fortune selling his invention to the British military, thousands of the bags now line the roads around this camp, and almost every other in the country.

The other ubiquitous building block of the city is the shipping container, the sort you see on travelling on the backs of trains, trucks or the decks of ships at ports around the world. There are now 10,000 shipping containers at Bastion, almost all of them brought in by road through Pakistan, after being shipped from Europe or America to Karachi. There are not that many that it is estimated it could take decades to take them all away again.

Rather than bringing in water supplies from elsewhere, the British set up a water-bottling plant on site, drawing the water from the two existing boreholes. The plastic bottles are made at the plant, which provides one million litres a week for Bastion, as well as many of the other smaller bases and checkpoints across Helmand province.

Most of the fresh food is flown in, with the rest coming by road. There is a central warehouse where most of it is stored – it is said to be the second-biggest building in the whole of Afghanistan. With between 20,000 and 30,000 people on the base at any one time, the quantities needed to feed everyone are vast - 27 tonnes of salad and fruit come in every week alone. Convoys of trucks, with armoured support, thunder out of the camp most days to supply other bases, often leaving in the middle of the night to minimise the disruption to the villages and towns that they rumble through.

The base has become so big that it has eight incinerators and a burn pit to get rid of the rubbish. The camp also has its own bus service, fire station and a police force. There are on-site laws and regulations too. One of them is the speed limit – 24kph

(15mph). It is enforced by officers with speed cameras, who can leap out from behind containers, or from inside ditches, to catch anyone flouting the rules. Anyone caught speeding more than three times is banned from driving on the base. Though the limit is quite low, many of the military vehicles are so big, and the dust they churn up so blinding, that it is dangerous for them to be going any faster.

There aren't any pavements at Bastion, or street lights, so walking around at night can be perilous without a torch. The airport is busy day and night. It deals with around 2,980,000 pieces of freight a month, including 73,000 pallets of mail.

There isn't much in the way of nightlife in the Camp, less the air-conditioned gyms that become regular haunts for many – there is a Pizza Hut that trades from inside a converted shipping container. Customers can even sit outside on pub-style benches. There is also a bar next door to the Pizza Hut called Heroes, which has giant TV screens showing news channels from the UK.

While the airport is the hub for flights in and out of the country, the heliport is busier. Every day, RAF Chinook, Sea King and Merlin helicopters run like buses, ferrying troops to and from the base. They are responsible for the bulk of the 600 movements undertaken across Helmand every day. There are also the Apaches and Lynx helicopters that go out with them to offer top cover and also go out on a wide range of missions offering fire support to troops on the ground.

One of the most surreal sights in the city is its Afghan village, a replica built by the British Army Engineers. It has a small number of local residents who tend to a bread oven, riding motorbikes and selling food at a market. The idea of it is to give soldiers a better feel for what to expect when they go on patrol. There is also a training area designed to help identify IEDs. They have been set up so soldiers learn; they can also be taught about the different techniques for planting IEDs, and how the villagers might be trying to warn them of their whereabouts. If an Afghan has stopped using a bridge to cross a stream or a river, there is often a reason and these are the subtle points that we all pick up out on patrol.

On a dark September night just after 10pm in Camp Bastion, an explosion echoed across the Helmand desert from the east. A two-metre hole had been blasted high in the razor-wire-topped wall surrounding what was thought to be one of the most impregnable military camps on earth. Fifteen fighters dressed in American army uniforms and armed with assault rifles and rocket-propelled grenades raced through the gap. They ran 150 metres and skirted a blast wall to run out onto a runway, bright under security lights.

Alongside it were 10 canvas hangars containing Harrier jets. These Taliban attackers, a very well drilled and cohesive unit of men, divided into three teams opened fire.

One group began shooting at the group of Marine Corps pilots and mechanics working on the AV-8B aircraft. The commander, Lieutenant-Colonel Christopher Raible, who always went and visited the hangars around 10pm every day, had to pull out his 9mm pistol so he could take on the attacking force. He had little chance against the intruder's superior rifle firepower and he was killed along with a mechanic, Sergeant Bradley Atwell. Nine other Marines were wounded in the attack.

The second group of Taliban fighters managed to destroy three refuelling stations. A third party then headed for the aircraft. The AV-8B Harriers had only arrived at the base in July – they have become hated by the Taliban for their deadly efficiency. Becoming just as hated as the Apache and A10. The attackers had time to plant explosives on several of the planes and others were hit with RPGs.

It was the single most destructive strike on a NATO base in the Afghan war. There is no doubt it was an astonishing raid - one that David Stirling himself would have been proud of. It was reminiscent of the raids carried out in 1941 in the African desert. You could say they almost copied those audacious raids in many ways and carried this raid out to great effect.

One senior officer even said, "It was like a textbook SF attack"

As the Marines came under attack at Bastion, motion detector alarms went off in the security command post. RAF 51 Squadron, which was in charge of protection; dispatched a 15-strong force in armoured Jackal patrol vehicles

The British took an estimated 12 minutes to get to the attack after the alarm was raised and various sensors had gone off. The 12 minutes it took was simply due to the size of Camp Bastion with its 27 miles of perimeter fence.

With the 15-strong RAF squad and marines stood their ground until a further 120 NATO soldiers were in action. However, the Taliban dodged between blast walls, and their American uniforms caused confusion.

The ensuing firefight was so fierce that the RAF troops alone fired over 10,000 rounds. The battle raged for almost four hours until a British Apache helicopter gunship ended it by finishing the Taliban off, with some 30mm cannon fire as they tried to escape across open ground. By daybreak 14 Taliban were dead and one was wounded and captured.

The fear was that the Taliban had created their own special operations unit to infiltrate highly protected facilities. The suspected masterminds was thought to be the Haqqani network, notorious militants based in Pakistan. The Haqqanis were set up in Afghanistan in the mid-1970s and were helped by the CIA and

Pakistan's Inter-Services Intelligence agency against the Soviet in the 1980s. According to US military commanders, it is "the most resilient enemy network" and one of the biggest threats to the U.S. -led NATO forces and the Afghan government.

For the raid on Camp Bastion, the Haqqani network, even had some detailed maps of Bastion as well as the correct US uniforms. That was subsequently used in the raid on Camp Bastion and led to the confusion of trying to identify who was friend and who was foe.

The Taliban must have had some form of inside information, possible information that had come from Afghan army defectors.

A local Taliban commander who gave his name as Abdul Bari told a leading Newspaper that planning began a month before the raid - when a senior Haqqani network officer asked for 20 volunteers to become suicide bombers. They were then trained in Pakistan in preparation for the raid.

The commander said an Afghan Taliban had gone to Pakistan to collect the militants a few days before the attack. They had spent two nights in a safe house in Afghanistan before striking. The Haqqanis specialise in co-ordinated attacks and were behind the assault on the US embassy in Kabul. Despite close links with Pakistan's military intelligence, the Haqqanis have been designated as a terrorist outfit by the Obama administration.

CHAPTER NINE – SEA HARRIER

Falklands War

The Royal Navy's introduction of the Sea Harrier came more than ten years after the RAF had started operating the Harrier GR1. On 1 April 1980, 800 Naval Air Squadron (NAS) formed at RNAS Yeovilton, Somerset, followed by 801 NAS on 26 February 1981. After the commissioning of the brand-new 'through-deck cruiser' HMS Invincible, 800 NAS embarked for its first major deployment in September 1980. Also deployed was 801 NAS on the ageing conventional aircraft carrier HMS Hermes. When Argentine forces invaded the Falklands on 2 April 1982, some Sea Harriers were still lacking their Blue Fox radars, and none of them had been cleared to carry BAe Sea Eagle anti-ship missiles. However, the Sea Harrier was operational, albeit with limited capabilities, in the nick of time for the Falklands conflict. It had entered service and become available at a key time and was now going to get the chance to prove itself in battle. The Falklands War (Spanish: Guerra de las Malvinas), also known as the Falklands Conflict, Falklands Crisis was a ten-week war between Argentina and the United Kingdom over two British overseas territories in the South Atlantic: the Falkland Islands and South Georgia and the South Sandwich Islands.

The war began on Friday 2 April 1982, when Argentina invaded the Falkland Islands, then the following day, invaded South

Georgia and the South Sandwich Islands in an attempt to establish their sovereignty it had long claimed over them. In response, the British government on 5 April 1982, dispatched a naval task force to engage the Argentine Navy and its Air Force, before making an amphibious assault on the islands. The conflict lasted 74 days and ended with the Argentine surrender on 14 June 1982, returning the islands to British control. In total, 649 Argentine military personnel, 255 British military personnel and three Falkland Islanders died during the hostilities. Tensions over the Islands have not ceased and Argentina still claims that they should be handed back. However, the Islanders want to remain British. The underlying reason is thought to be linked with oil deposits for Argentina's continued claim on the Islands.

The British Task Force that was sent to the South Atlantic to battle with Argentine forces could not have been as effective without the Harrier. Without the Harrier, the outcome of the war could have been different. At the same time, despite its relative maturity, the RAF's Harrier GR3 was only cleared to fire its 30mm Aden cannon and drop 1,000lb (454kg) bombs along with BL-755 cluster weapons. It did not have clearance for the new third-generation AIM-9L Sidewinder, laser-guided bombs, or Shrike anti-radiation missiles.

In order to provide more air power, No. 1 Squadron flew fourteen Harrier GR3s nonstop (some 4,000 miles) from the UK to Ascension Island in the South Atlantic. The Harriers made the trip in nine hours, refueling in midair five times. The First Sea Lord, Adm Sir Henry Leach after the war stated *"Without the Sea Harrier there would have been no Task Force. Operating from carriers proved the concept of V/STOL air operations in independent amphibious operations."*

The Task Force had in total 28 Sea Harriers, 14 RAF Harrier GR3s, together with 175 helicopters. The actual air war began on 1 May, when an early bombing raid on Port Stanley airfield by an RAF Vulcan bomber flying from Ascension Island was followed by a dawn attack by twelve Sea Harriers operating from HMS Hermes. The Sea Harriers mainly operated in the air combat role, whilst the GR3s focused on ground attack. The Sea Harriers took a toll of incoming Argentinian aircraft that was quite remarkable in the circumstances undertaking 1,435 sorties.

Sea Harriers and Harrier GR3s operated from Royal Navy aircraft carriers, which remained a considerable distance offshore to stay out of range of the highly effective Exocet anti-shipping missiles real. The downside of this meant that the Harriers are a much larger ferry distance to their area of operation. This reduced the time they were able to loiter and be able to support ground troops. As soon as the British Invasion Force at San Carlos had moved inland a forward operating base (FOB) was built by the Royal Engineers at a site north-west of Port San Carlos settlement. The FOB was constructed of aluminium decking, but was only half the size than had been originally planned due to the loss of the Atlantic Conveyor. The Atlantic Conveyor along with much needed helicopters also had the extra materials for the engineers to build harrier runways. The Atlantic Conveyor had been lost after being struck by two Exocet missiles on 25 May 1982 and was badly burnt and had to subsequently be abandoned with 12 men killed. The ship eventually sank whilst under tow on 28 May 1982. As the last resting place of the remains of those who died, the wreck is designated as a protected place under the Protection of Military Remains Act 1986. There is a memorial to the Atlantic Conveyor in, Trinity Gardens, Tower Hill, London. With the loss of materials the landing strip was narrowed and ended up 850ft long with a turning loop at one end. It could cope with only four aircraft. The runway was first used on 5 June 1982 by a Sea Harrier, it was then continuously used by the RAF and RN as required, aircraft and pilots remaining overnight on occasions. It was known as RAF Port San Carlos to the RAF, or HMS Sheathbill to the RN, but was more usually referred to as 'Sid's Strip' after the commanding officer, Sqn Ldr 'Sid' Morris. The RAF's Harrier GR3s played an invaluable role in taking over much of the highly dangerous ground/ surface attack mission, and made 126 operational sorties, with a loss of four GR3s. One GR3 was shot down by shoulder fired missile, in Port Howard on

21 May, another GR3 was hit by anti-aircraft fire on 27 May over Goose Green and the third GR3 hit by ground fire near Port Stanley on 30 May. The fourth and final GR3A loss was in landing accident on 8 June.

Although no Sea Harriers were destroyed in air combat, two Sea Harriers were lost to ground fire - hit by anti-aircraft fire during the 4 May attack on Goose Green and by a Roland missile during the 1 June attack on Port Stanley. The four to accidents were due to two 801 Sqn Sea Harriers colliding whilst on CAP over the task force on 6 May 1982. One Sea Harrier from 800 Squadron crashed during takeoff from Hermes on 24 May and one Sea Harrier from 801Squadron slid off the deck in bad weather on 29 May. In total the Sea Harrier squadrons shot down 20 Argentine aircraft. Out of the total Argentine air losses, 28% were shot down by Harriers. The failure of the Argentinian fighters to shoot down a Sea Harrier was through a variety of factors. The Mirage III and Dagger jets were considerably faster than the Harrier. However, they lacked the manoeuvrability of the Harrier - this proved to be decisive in air to air combat between the RAF and Argentine Air Force. The Harrier also employed the latest AIM-9L Sidewinder missiles and the Blue Fox radar, along with British pilots having superior air-combat training.

The conflict was short, and it revealed some shortcomings in both Harrier variants. On the other hand, it demonstrated beyond any doubt the unique operational versatility of the family and its abilities as an effective fighter and ground attack aircraft. Without the foresight of the naval planners who had stubbornly fought for the Sea Harrier, the Falklands might well have been given up to Argentina without a fight. After hostilities ceased, a Harrier Detachment of six GR3s, together with two Sea Harriers, was established at Port Stanley, becoming No. 1453 Flight in August 1983. The Harriers and Sea Harriers returned to the UK once Mount Pleasant airfield was opened on 12 May 1985 and RAF McDonnell Douglas Phantom II took over the role.

On 7 December 1988, the MOD awarded BAE a contract to upgrade the surviving fleet of FRS1 Sea Harriers to FRS2 standard, beginning in October 1990, together with ten new-build FRS2s. Delivery of the FRS2 began in 1994. It was during delivery that the designation was changed to FA2 to reflect the equal importance of the Sea Harrier's fighter role along with its ground or surface attack. The total number of upgrades was later increased to sixteen and then later to eighteen. The main equipment change was the replacement of Blue Fox radar with the GEC-Ferranti Blue Vixen track-while-scan pulse Doppler radar. This gave the Sea Harrier an all-weather look-down, shoot-down capability, together with the ability to engage multiple targets simultaneously. The Pegasus Mk 104 used in the FRS1 was replaced with the Mk106, the naval version of the 21,550lbf

Mk105 used in the Harrier GR7 and later GR9, which had an extra 200 lbf of thrust.

The cockpit was modernised, with a new heads up display, and two-function displays. An improved HOTAS (hands-on throttle and stick) controls the same as fitted to the GR7. The Sea Harrier was also the first European combat aircraft to be equipped with the AIM-120 AMRAAM anti-aircraft missile.

The FA2 had an improved IFF (identification friend or foe), expendable radar decoys that could be fired from the chaff/ flare dispensers, a handheld Garmin 100 GPS navigation receiver mounted in the cockpit, and the latest AIM-9M Sidewinders. Five of the Navy's two-seat Harriers were upgraded to T8 standard, in line with the FA2, in 1994. The first operational FA2 unit to form was 801 NAS at RNAS Yeovilton on 5 October 1994. Once operational the FA2 was involved in the monitoring of shipping to enforce the arms blockade (Operation Decisive Enhancement), the denial of fixed-wing air activity in the Balkans as part of the international peacekeeping efforts and missions in Sierra Leone. Although the Royal Navy Sea Harriers proved to be very effective and they established their ability to operate from Royal Navy carrier decks in all conditions, the aircraft itself became costly to maintain and needed comprehensive upgrades to keep it viable after 2005. A decision was reached in 2002 by the UK Government to withdraw the Sea Harrier from service and re-equip the two RN squadrons with Harrier GR7A/9s. Sea Harriers made their final flight on 28 March 2006 at RNAS Yeovilton and were stored pending disposal.

With the end of operations for the Harrier fleet in 2010 the Royal Navy was left without aircraft or a carrier. Although, the purchase of the STOVL F-35B to be operated from the Royal Navy's new Queen Elizabeth class aircraft carrier, will give the Royal Navy fixed wing air-power once more. 809 NAS was reformed in September 2013 to become the first Fleet Air Arm squadron to be equipped with the F-35 Lightning II. The squadron will operate alongside the reformed 617 'Dambusters' Squadron of the Royal Air Force. 809 NAS had originally been disbanded on 17 December 1982. 617 squadron was disbanded on 28 March 2014 with both being reformed and active with the F35 by 2016.

CHAPTER TEN – RECOIL SIX

"Recoil Six Four, Crowbar," a distant sounding voice crackled over the radio. The JTAC followed this with a position, call sign and frequency of the unit that had requested urgent assistance. I immediately identified the location on the map display on my left hand TV screen. Myself and Fuzz altered course and our increased speed. At around 430 knots and heading straight towards the mountains of the Pakistani border, I dialled in the frequency and called up the unit's radio operator. "Jaguar One Two, this is Recoil Six Four." "Recoil Six Four, Jaguar One Two, roger. Ready for fighter check-in." I quickly passed him all our details and finished with our current position. "Estimate minutes four to overhead target."

We had been called in for a classic interdiction mission, a Taliban convoy of opium was trying to make its way out of Afghanistan and into Pakistan. A Special Forces patrol was watching their route out, but did not have the manpower or firepower to take the convoy out and an airstrike was the only viable alternative. We had the coordinates, but it was a moving target without headlights moving under the cover of darkness. We had our NVGs (Night Vision Goggles). The trucks will have most likely have come from Helmand. Helmand is believed to be one of the largest producers of Opium in the world, with nearly 75% of the world's supply coming from the region. Opium is the Taliban's biggest source of income and helps pay for the Afghan war.

It was a convoy of three trucks and a pickup truck, snaking their way across Afghanistan. On the pickup truck were four armed Taliban fighters wearing dish dashes.

Through my NVGs the ground below me took on a green hue and I could clearly see he road below, I would use this as my reference point as we sped towards the convoy. I still found, though, that I lost some of my spatial awareness with the original NVGs. The NVGs work with the FLIR (Forward-Looking Infra-Red) systems, which when used with pilot's night-vision goggles, provide us with the capability for night-time operations. These are fully-integrated with all the systems, meaning the way we do business by night is exactly the same as during the day, including flying at low level.

For the final six months, we operated with a Helmet Mounted Cueing System (HMCS). This allowed the pilot to quickly identify coordinates on the ground using a red diamond which was projected over it on a reticule placed over the right eye. This really was an excellent tool in increasing your spatial awareness and takes away the need to spend vital minutes using binoculars to identify features from a map.

NVGs and FLIR changed the way the Harrier operated along with the Paveway IV. With the Paveway not only can the bomb be guided to its target using a laser from either the aircraft, through the Sniper Targeting Pod, or from the ground, it can also be delivered onto precise GPS coordinates. At 500lb, it's also a lighter weapon when compared to some of the more traditional 1,000lb variants. Another advantage with this weapon is that the fuse is cockpit-programmable, allowing the pilot to tailor the effect of the weapon depending on the target and the requirement of the boots on the ground. It can, for instance, penetrate through layers of concrete before exploding, thus allowing us to accurately target the precise part of the building to be destroyed. I got the harrier lined up, my plan was to drop a Pavway on the first vehicle whilst Fuzz went for the second, the third we could hopefully take out with a few rockets. However, the third lorry may well try to get off the road and into the desert in the hope of fleeing. We dropped down to 6000 feet and began our run, as soon as I got the target in sight I got it locked into the targeting system and at the right point hit the pickle bottom. The Paveway dived onto its target and hit it with devastating effect, moments later the second truck was obliterated. I went into a tight turn, with the third lorry in my six, pulling a high g-turn to get back round for a final run on the third truck. Fuzz would follow in on my tail and act as a spotter helping reduce my activity level for a busy attack The third truck had swerved to avoid the first two burning trucks and just carried on with its Taliban escort. The four men were standing up with AK47s in hand as they came back into view.

I had already switched to rockets and got the truck lined up in my HUD. I went into a shallow dive before releasing six rockets, which streaked off in front of me, before finding their target and stopping the truck in its tracks. With the third truck taken out, Fuzz finished off the pickup truck, just so it did not pose any threat to the Special Forces, now a mile behind us. A night mission is always a very tiring experience, the dark does hide so much and you have to be aware of the still very busy sky in Afghanistan, especially around Kabul and Kandahar with nearly as many night flights as daytime flights.

CHAPTER ELEVEN – JOINT FORCE HARRIER

Joint Force Harrier (JFH), was established on 1 April 2000. JFH brought RAF Harriers and RN Sea Harriers into a common command structure as part of a Joint Rapid Deployment Force. With plans well under way for the Sea Harrier to move to RAF Cottesmore to join the RAF Harriers, it was announced on 28 February 2002 that JFH was to become an all-ground-attack force. The Sea Harriers were to be retired completely in early 2006 due to the cost of upgrading them and the GR7/9 being able to fulfil their role. In 2000, Harriers operating from HMS Illustrious were involved in combat missions over Sierra Leone. The RAF Harrier force was later involved in Kosovo, and again in Iraq (Operation Telic) in 2003, when twenty-three RAF Harriers took part in the campaign, being based inland in Kuwait. Maverick missiles were used successfully by a small number of Harrier GR7s involved in Operation Telic, although this was not a standard capability at the time. Crews from all of the RAF Harrier squadrons have been based in Afghanistan since September 2004, operating six GR7s in support of International Security Assistance Force (ISAF) from Kandahar airfield. Improvements and modifications to the RAF's Harriers continued. The GR7 received an upgraded ad more powerful Pegasus engine and became the GR7A. The capability of the

GR7 had been limited by its engine, the Pegasus 105, particularly in high temperatures and during shipboard operations. Airframe issues were dealt with by BAE Systems in Harrier Modification Programme 3. GR7s being modified to enable them to be fitted with the yet more powerful Pegasus 107 engine that provides 3,000lb more thrust than the 21,500lb thrust the Mk105 it replaces. The extra power gives the resulting GR9s improved hover, allows for extended sorties and gives improved hot and high performance, as well as enhancing carrier-based operations. The Harrier GR9 also had an Integrated Weapons Programme (IWP) enhancement, which brought together a number of discrete weapon systems, including MBDA's Brimstone anti-armour 'fire-and-forget' missiles, Raytheon's Paveway IV precision-guided bomb and IR/ TV-guided versions of the Raytheon AGM-65 Maverick. The GR9 had no guns fitted, but the retained pods from the previous Arden cannon actually help provide additional lift on take-off and landing. TIALD pods, which provided laser designation, were installed in place of one of the old gun blisters. Also included is the Successor Identification Friend or Foe (SIFF) system, which makes the aircraft less vulnerable in an operational environment. The work was carried out at RAF Cottesmore, run by BAE Systems as part of the Joint Availability Support Solution project. The programme also added a full digital cockpit and a new open-architecture computer, GPS navigation and secure communications.

JFH received its first upgraded Harrier GR9 from BAE Systems in late 2005. It was delivered to No. 1 (F) Squadron at RAF Cottesmore as part of a £ 500m programme that saw sixty Harrier GR7/ 7As, upgraded to GR9/ 9A and eleven T10 trainers modified to T12 standard. The first T12 flew in January 2005. The improved trainers also had the IWP upgrades, but not the higher-power engine.

Joint Force Harrier provided the air support for British troops as part of a NATO force in the south of Afghanistan after they moved into the troubled Kandahar province in 2005 until 2009. With the personnel changing every few months, 800 NAS took over from No. 4 Squadron, RAF, in September 2006 and was soon in action for the first time with Harrier GR7As. They helped ground forces deter insurgency activity and, where necessary, attacked carefully selected Taleban targets. The fully constituted Joint Force of two RAF and two RN Harrier squadrons at RAF Cottesmore and the Harrier Joint Operational Conversion Unit at RAF Wittering became fully operational in April 2007.

All four squadrons had twelve pilots which moved from the GR7 to the GR9/ 9A and T12. The RN squadrons continued to fulfil most of the naval tasks, but the benefit of JFH. Was that the two services operated the same aircraft type within a common structure and were capable of operating both on land and at sea. In modern military planning, mobility and flexibility have become key words.

CHAPTER TWELVE – AV-8B

17 January 1991 Kuwait

As the sun rose the warmth of the sun hit the cold desert floor after another cool night. Nearby in the border town of Khafji in Kuwait, an Iraqi artillery battery was responding to coalition forces raids on Baghdad with 122mm shells. As the sun rose it helped to give the Iraqi gunners a better view on what they were firing at. Which was a nearby oil refinery and US Marine Corps mobile units - dug in along the border. The Marines had already radioed in for air support to neutralize the Iraqi artillery. The first aircraft to get on station was a twin turboprop OV-A10 Bronco from VMO-1. The pilot of Bronco was with the FAC (Forward Air Controller) circling the artillery position at 5,000 feet doing a recce of the situation. They were both able to quickly get a grid reference for the artillery in preparation for an air strike. Four V8B Harrier IIs were already en-route to the scene from the VMA-211 'Tomcats' having been alerted whilst on patrol.

The AV-8Bs were based at King Abdul Aziz airfield (100 miles from the Kuwaiti border) in Saudi Arabia. Each of the AV8Bs was armed with four MK83 low drag bombs on the inner pylons and a single AIM-9M Sidewinder missile on the outer pylon. Finally a GAU-12A 'Equalizer' five barrel 25mm Gattling gun housed in an under fuselage pod. Cruising at 20,000 feet the four AV-8Bs were closing in fast onto the Bronco's current position, which had now moved over the Gulf to allow the four AV-8Bs a clear run on the target. The Iraqi gunners were still firing away with their 120mm shells spewing out of their artillery at a fearsome rate. As the AV-8Bs closed in on Khafji, each pilot checked to see that the master arm had been set to on and the Hughs ARBS (Angle Rate Bombing System) in the nose of the plane was working correctly. Their HUDs displayed the waypoint to the target area. As the AV-8Bs got close, they could see smoke at their 11 o'clock position. The lead AV-8B then began a shallow descent to 15,000 feet.

The FAC meanwhile had worked out a suitable attack profile that would allow the AV8Bs to hit the target from behind and then do a tactical pull out after weapons release, in the direction of friendly territory. This was done to minimize the chance of a damaged jet coming down in enemy territory. The AV-8Bs began their attack run after confirming they had a visual on the enemy position. Below they could now see the muzzle flashes from the artillery piece. The four AV-8Bs split into pairs before rolling in on the target, maintaining a 5 second separation between each AV-8B. Each pair attacked from different directions flying downward at a 45 degree angle. Each jet was travelling at approximately 525 knots as they descended. It was known through intelligence that most Iraqi units carried a SAM-7, a shoulder mounted ground to air SAM. As a precaution each jet dispensed chaff during their dive onto the target as well as dropping flares as they pulled out. With the ARBS locked onto the target, it calculated the exact time for weapon release. The first AV-8B pilot guided by a small cross on his HUD generated by the CCIP (Constantly Computed Impact Point) over the 120mm artillery that was still firing. At 6000 feet the pilot released his bombs before pulling back and into a high G pull up and away from the target. The pullup manoeuvre exerted around five G on both the pilot and the AV-8B. Before making some evasive manoeuvres and heading back towards Saudia Arabia. The other AV8Bs followed suit, leaving the wrecked Iraqi artillery behind and climbing back up to 15,000 feet.

This attack on 17 January 1991 was the first time the AV-8Bs had been used in anger in war. The AV-8A and later AV-8B having had nearly twenty years of peaceful service prior to the Gulf Conflict and Operation Desert Storm. The 88 AV-8Bs the US Marine Corps had in theatre; went on to undertake 3380 sorties and drop 5.95 million pounds of ordnance. The first AV-8B was lost in combat on 28 January 28 an AV-8B was shot down by anti-aircraft artillery (AAA). The pilot a Captain Michael C. Berryman was captured. He was subsequently released on 6 March 1991. In total five AV-8Bs were lost during Operation Desert Storm, four to enemy fire and one, to a training accident.

The Marines Corps AV-8B fleet is to remain in service until 2025, owing to delays with the F-35B and the fact that the Harriers have more service life left in them than the USMC F/A-18 Hornets.

CHAPTER THIRTEEN – STORMY WEATHER

It was late morning and about 90 troops from the 4th Infantry Brigade Combat Team, 1st Infantry Division were making their way towards an RV (rendezvous point) after completing a mission against the Taliban overnight in eastern Afghanistan. Their destination was a flat section of mountain ridgeline that was about a mile above the large valley below. The ridgeline was surrounded by 12,000 foot mountains that made it look and feel like they were in another world.

Two A10s were on station high above acting as over-watch, ready to provide close air support at a moment's notice. Fuzz had I, been requested to go in as back up if the need arose, but for now were on a recce patrol. Using the Digital Joint Reconnaissance Pod (DJPR): Most people would imagine that our time in Afghanistan was all about dropping bombs, this could not have been further from the truth. For the vast majority of the time we were tasked with taking high-resolution imagery for the ground commanders and their soldiers. This could be anything from looking at changes to patterns of life, building construction and layout, or in the hunt for IEDs. The good news with the DJPR, was that it did not affect our weapon load-out, so we could swing from either a reconnaissance mission to Close Air Support at the drop of a hat, depending on the ever changing circumstances of the war on the ground. Reconnaissance is as important as Close Air Support in many ways, without intelligence on the enemy's location and strength is virtually impossible to plan any form of attacks. We frequently got airborne carrying camera pods and, in the absence of any close air support being required. We would be tasked with photographing a particular area where it was known or believed that the Taliban might be located. Although, the DJPR imagery is in black-and-white, the resolution was exceptionally high. With the correct equipment, 3D images could be developed and intricate graphics produced, providing a valuable source of intelligence.

Along with the usual weapon load, we had on either side, two big fuel tanks under each wing and a targeting pod under ZG477s belly. We had initially been briefed to fly a tactical reconnaissance and intelligence-gathering sortie, we both had reconnaissance pods slung from the centreline station. However, as events unfolded, we would not stay on recce for long…

As the 4th Infantry Brigade had made their way back to the RV, they noticed Taliban forces were in the area and made best use of the ridgeline and natural cover to hide their progress. The Taliban had by now become alerted to the presence of the 4th and were directing inaccurate fire towards the US troops. The US troops started to take cover and returned fire, just as dark, stormy clouds began to form above them, along with a much stronger wind. We were alerted to the situation via JTAC and told to start heading to the area. The winds, were reported to be getting stronger by the minute. This would mean the planned pick-up time would need to be moved up to avoid the worst of the weather. The two Hogs already on over-watch also needed relief as they would be getting low on fuel and weapons with conditions still getting worse, the Black Hawks and our Harriers made our way to the RV. The weather made what was already a hazardous mountainous area even more so. One particular mountain range, just north, was known to provide the ideal environment for a very dangerous kind of storm.

As we made our way to the area, the ground battle continued, with the existing Hogs trying their best to target enemy positions and reduce the rate of incoming fire as the US Infantry did their best to hold their position. However, unbeknown to them, a massive storm was building above the 12,000-foot-high northern mountain range; this would bring its own assault on the troops and make for difficult flying conditions. The combination of afternoon temperatures topping 100 degrees and the expanding storm front meant a KC-135, which was due to fuel a pair of F-16s heading to the area, had to divert away. This would in turn reduce the amount of time we could spend at the target area, as would now have a longer distance to travel to meet up with the KC-135.

The weather was still deteriorating as we arrived on station and the clouds had got thicker and much lower, which meant we would have to fly lower. This in turn would mean we would burn more fuel. It was not long before JTAC gave us our first target just below the ridgeline on which the US troops were holding firm. The Taliban was still pouring into the area and the ensuing fire fight was becoming fiercer with every minute. I knew time was of the essence and that we would need to refuel very soon. The best way round this was for one of us to stay on station whilst the other went to refuel. I sent Fuzz off to refuel first, hoping he would be back in time before I ran too low.

As my wingman departed, the storm seemed to increase in size and swept over the mountains from the north. Fuzz had to find a flight path around the giant system as it was too high to fly over, but soon discovered that the refuelling tanker had moved again from its scheduled position to the other side of the storm. At the same time, I was about to begin my first attack when the storm finally broke into the valley. The storm's pressure was building layers, which collapsed when it hit the valley, causing microburst. A microburst is a localized column of air which sinks. This in turn produces damaging divergent and straight-line winds at the surface, which are similar in some ways to a tornado, and normally have convergent damage. A microburst is deadly for aircraft and was the cause of Delta Airlines Flight 191 and a

Lockheed L-1011-335-1 TriStar to crash in Dallas on 2nd August 1985, killing 137 passengers. A microburst-induced wind shear had forced the plane into the ground. Pilot error was also cited as an additional factor in the crash. For me, a potential microburst added to the danger of flying low in a mountainous region, the map display being my secondary reference after mk1 eyeball. The weather was severe enough to pull the whole attack from our point of view, but this would have meant US troops being put in even greater danger and potentially being overran. The hope was that the storm would subside as quickly as it had started. For now I had a job to do in what was one of the most challenging sorties of my career.

The US troops remained under increasing fire as the torrential downpour finally arrived, along with torrents of sand mixed with water. All that, plus lightning and a very strong wind, engulfed them. With the storm raging on, the vast number of Taliban fighters in the area, moved towards the middle of the US Forces' position, cutting it in two. At the same time; larger calibre fire was being directed from a mountain across the valley as the full Taliban ambush came into effect. The US troops were now in a fierce fire fight, fighting for their lives as rounds sent small chunks of rock flying off in all directions as it became more and more accurate. Finally, the US troops took their first casualty and then the medic tending to the injured soldier was also hit and mortally wounded. With every minute, the situation for both ZG477 and the US troops was getting more and more difficult.

I was forced to an even lower altitude on each attack run as visibility decreased. Increasing the potential to be hit by small and medium arms fire as well as any SAMs. I could barely see out of his cockpit as the rain lashed against the windshield and ran off, causing very poor visibility. Think of travelling along the motorway at 70mph in a torrential downpour and triple the speed. The storm meant I was also burning even more fuel and, at the same time, running low on rockets and bombs after quite a few passes over various enemy positions. Fuzz had managed to find the KC-135 and take on some fuel. Halfway through, I had to request that he return to me as soon as possible. Radio communication was becoming increasingly difficult as the weather was causing more communication problems than usual; this was later found to have been made worse by a recent solar flare. I continued to provide close air support whilst dodging rounds and flying in near-zero visibility at times, until I was out of rockets. I was now running very short on fuel, and my Bingo fuel warning started to wail. This left me with no choice but to return to Kandahar after a fuel top up at the KC-135. I passed on my update to Fuzz, who was eight miles away, as best I could with the poor comms during to atmospheric conditions. The Taliban was rapidly gaining ground and the US troops were taking casualties, including the JTAC communicating with both the Hogs that were on their way and our Harrier's.

It was some of the worst weather I have ever flown in and the valley now looked completely different to when I had arrived. Fuzz was now taking up the fight and knew he had to press on. With visibility so low, Fuzz fired off a rocket to mark the position he was going to target and confirm with the JTAC that it was correct. Finally, two more Hogs arrived overhead to help out. The two Hogs got the US troops to move further up the ridgeline so they could go in and make a co-ordinated attack. Hundreds of 30mm shells and rockets hit the enemy positions; they were quite tightly packed, making them an easy target now that the US troops had put some distance between them. After a few final attack runs, Fuzz's ammunition ran out; it was his time to depart and return to Kandahar.

The two other Hogs remained on station, reducing enemy activity enough for a medevac helicopter to begin picking up the most seriously injured troops. The two Hogs continued to pummel enemy positions as more and more troops were picked up by helicopter after a 13 hour fire fight. It was beginning to get dark as the sun set behind the Afghan mountains when the final troops were pulled out.

After landing, I had an instant pounding headache for the intensity and concentration of the flying I had just done. ZG477 had got me home safely and ran fault free under a very difficult sortie in terms of flying conditions. Once again showing how the Harrier could keep up with the venerable A10 in danger close air support.

.

CHAPTER FOURTEEN – FINAL BOW

A 540lb-pound bomb dropped from a Harrier can take a group of Taliban out in an instance thus ending a fire fight. However, accuracy is the key, as the same bomb dropped slightly off target could lead to a blue on blue. This margin of error is the difference between helping the troops on the ground and making a horrific mistake. Close air support in Afghanistan is more often than not undertaken at 'danger close' distances. The wrong co-ordinates from JTAC or even us pilots getting them wrong could cause friendly fatalities. That responsibility is always present and it is the pilot dropping the bomb or firing the rockets that shoulders the overall responsibility. You need to know and understand the rules of engagement and the effects of each and every weapon you fire.

One A-10 pilot mistook, what was just a trash fire, for a Taliban position and ended up strafing a group of US troops battling Taliban forces. The strike killed one soldier and injured dozens, putting even greater scrutiny on how Hog pilots, as well as the rest of us pilots involved in close air support missions, avoided fratricide. One issue is that there are not enough Air Force controllers on the ground to meet this need, and some allied countries don't even have any. There is also a discrepancy with the kit they carry, as some NATO controllers do not have the newest and latest equipment. Other times equipment failures either on the ground or in the air, can lead to judgement calls needing to be made, to fire or not to fire. Communications can and does fail, be it a radio on the ground or even in the air. Often it is almost a balancing act of protecting friendly soldiers on the ground from the Taliban whilst not wanting them to be caught up by friendly fire from the air. The selection of a weapon and its yield is another crucial area and we need to know the potential effects of each and every weapon we fire.

The Taliban would often perform quick attacks or ambushes, and as soon as some form of air support was on station, they would retreat, usually back into a village where you could not drop a bomb or fire rockets for fear of civilian casualties. There is no point protecting civilians from the Taliban, only to go and kill a few with accidental friendly fire. The fallout, both in terms of propaganda and effects on the local populace is to higher price. After all we need to keep the local populace on our side.

The main mantra of the Afghan war is to remove extremists and prevent attacks on the Afghan people and their infrastructure. Then help Afghanistan to have its own independent and democratic government, along with security forces that can stop the Taliban taking back areas of Afghanistan. This has largely been achieved in some areas of Afghanistan. However, the size of Afghanistan most often means that the enemy has moved from one area to another more remote part of the country. It is still in an unstable and volatile state and with the final withdrawal of the last troops, what happens long term is very much in the mix. The government whilst gaining strength is still on a knife edge, as is the Afghan Army and security forces.

As for Harrier GR9, that both the Royal Navy and RAF flew in Afghanistan. It was arguably the best Close Air Support platform in the world. Previously it had been second to the Fairchild A-10 Thunderbolt II. The final GR9 upgrades brought it up to be on a par with the A10. Partly due to having a helmet-mounted cueing system. This meant Harrier pilots could look out at a target and instead of having to point a sensor at a target, you could just click a button on the throttle. This would then enter the target we were looking at directly into the weapon system. It made a huge difference to the speed in which a target could be acquired and a weapon selected and before being fired on target. The GR9 also got an upgrade of its self-defence suit. This all helped put the Harrier GR9 at the forefront of close air support. The A10 can take more punishment that is in no doubt. However, fully laden it fly's slower than a World War Two Spitfire at 240 knots. A Harrier fully laden could still fly at well over 400 knots, getting on station in a shorter time or in not far off half the time over the same distance. In the fast and dynamic world of close air support, that could mean the difference between life and death.

It was a sad and sudden demise of the GR9 in 2010. With the Tornado GR4, replacing its main role, along with the Typhoon.

As for the role that Joint Force Harrier undertook, it could perhaps be summarised as Shape, Clear, Hold and Build and this was achieved through a graduated response. It was through a mixture of Kinetic and Non-Kinetic effects; indeed, the non-kinetic effects was how the pilot often tried to resolve an unfolding situation.

Shaping can best be described as missions that undertook the role of Non-Traditional Information Surveillance and Reconnaissance (NTISR); in this respect the Harrier would use sensors to provide an overview of the battlefield. Equally, at times a mere presence where either through an audible of visual presence it could cause the Taliban to retreat. Finally, if the situation dictated, a deliberate 'surgical' strike might be called for, in order to provide ground forces with a tactical advantage by neutralizing a position or positions before or after a ground attack.

Clearing was where we brought the Harrier into the Close Air Support (CAS) role, providing Armed Overwatch. Utilising 'Shows of Force', the aim was to deter or disperse insurgents, or if that failed, then a Kinetic response could be brought to bear. The important point, is that this effect had to be Precise, Discriminate and Proportional, something that the Harrier became known for; if an effect could be achieved through firing one rocket, then that was what was delivered; equally, if soldiers' lives were at risk, then a weapon with a much higher yield might be more appropriate.

Holding is in many ways similar to Shaping, seeing the pattern of life monitored as well as a continued presence being maintained both audibly and visually. Equally, the continued hunt for IEDs would be undertaken whenever the sensors could be spared, all ensuring that the key ground gained was subsequently held. Soldier's live saved along with the local populous from the undiscriminating IED.

We also supported civilians by providing a presence on voting days, deterring the placement of IEDs, and a demonstration of a continued commitment by maintaining presence overhead. The JFH made a real difference during Operation Herrick; undoubtedly the lives of many Afghanistan civilians have been saved along with the lives of British and other coalition troops.

The Harrier statistics for Operation Herrick speak for themselves.

Missions flown: approx 4,500.

Sorties: 8,557.

Hours: 22,771.

Close Air Support missions: 2,000.

Average sortie time: 3 hours.

The Harrier made its mark in what was to be its final swan song in British service. It still lives on in the form of the AV8B, with most of the retired GR9s being sold to the US Marines to keep their AV8Bs flying until a projected 2030, showing how much life and value is still placed on the Harrier.

However, STOVL will be back with the RAF and Royal Navy, in the form of the F-35 Lightning II. The Lightning II is a supersonic, single-seat, single-engine, multi-role aircraft that can be configured for Close Air Support, tactical bombing and air-to-air combat. The F35A being of a conventional design and the F35B being the STOVL version and Rolls Royce has had a hand in the design the lift fan for the F35B.

Once in service it will be a capable aircraft that will take both the RAF and Royal Navy, well into the twenty-first century. Whilst it won't have the same character as the Harrier, akin to an LP record versus a CD. The CD may have less noise, be easier to navigate and use, but there is still something sterile and not quite natural about it. The digital element, making a subtle but discernible change from analogue.

As for ZG477, it can still be seen at RAF Cosford on permanent display since being retired in 2010. Entrance to RAF Cosford is free and well worth a visit for any family, aviation enthusiast or historian. Nothing beats seeing aircraft close up and being in awe of the size and complexity of their design.

GLOSSARY

AK47 – The AK47 Kalashnikov assault rifle more commonly known as the AK-47 or just AK (Avtomat Kalashnikova – 47, which translates to the Kalashnikov automatic rifle, model 1947), and its derivatives. It had been and still is with minor modifications, manufactured in dozens of countries, and has been used in hundreds of countries and conflicts since its introduction. The total number of the AK-type rifles made worldwide during the last 60 years is estimated at 90+ million. The AK47 is known for its simplicity of operation, ruggedness and maintenance, and unsurpassed reliability even in the most inhospitable of conditions.

Apache AH64 – The Bowing Apache AH64 is a twin engine attack helicopter with quite formidable firepower consisting of a fully movable 30mm cannon, rockets and Hellfire missiles stored in pods on the stubby wings.

AV8B – The AV8B was manufactured under licence by McDonnell Douglas and based on the Hawker Sidney Harrier jump jet. Capable of vertical or short takeoff and landing (V/STOL), the aircraft was designed in the late 1970s as an Anglo-American development of the British Hawker Siddeley Harrier. It first flew in 1978 and is now powered by a single Rolls-Royce F402-RR-408 (Mk 107) vectored-thrust turbofan.

Boeing C-17 Globemaster III is a large military transport aircraft. It was developed for the United States Air Force from the 1980s to the early 1990s, originally by McDonnell Douglas until Boeing took over McDonnell. It first flew on 15 September 1991 and entered service on 17 January 199. Powered by four Pratt & Whitney F117-PW-100 turbofans, each developing 40,440 lbf of thrust. The C-17 commonly performs strategic airlift missions, transporting troops and cargo throughout the world; additional roles include tactical airlift, medical evacuation and airdrop duties. It has a payload of 77,519 kg and is 174 feet long.

BvS 10 Viking is an all-terrain armoured vehicle produced by BAE Systems Land Systems Hagglunds of Sweden. This vehicle, referred to as the all-Terrain Vehicle (protected) - ATV(P) or Viking by the UK forces, was originally developed as a collaboration between industry - Hägglunds Vehicle AB - and the UK Ministry of Defence (MoD) on behalf of the Royal Marines.

C8 - The C8 was born out of the C7 when in 1984; Canada adopted a new 5.56 mm assault rifle. The C7 itself was based on a later version of the M16. To avoid research and design expenses, the Canadians simply purchased the license from USA for a new assault rifle, chambered for the latest 5.56 x 45 NATO ammunition. This was the Colt model 715, also known as the M16A1E1 rifle. Adopted as the C7, this rifle combined features from both earlier M16A1 rifles and the newest M16A2. Later on,

Diemaco (now Colt Canada) developed a short-barrelled carbine version, fitted with telescoped buttstock, which was designated the C8.

CH-47 Chinook - The CH-47 Chinook is an American helicopter built by Boeing with a tandem rotor design. It first flew in September 1961 and has gone through many changes since then. Originally powered by two Lycoming T55-GA-714A turboshaft engines. It has seen service around the world with the USAF, USMC, RAF in a variety of conflicts and wars. It is currently in service with 26 different countries and a total of 1179 have been built. The SAS uses a specially adapted 'Special Forces' version of the Chinook. Eight Chinook HC3s were ordered in 1995 as dedicated special forces helicopters, which were intended to be low-cost variants of the US Army's MH-47E. The HC3s include improved range, night vision sensors and navigation capability.

DShK – The DShK is a Russian heavy machine gun that came into service in 1938. It is gas operated, with a 12.7x109 mm calibre belt fed and air cooled machine gun. It can be used as an anti-aircraft gun mounted on a pintle. It is also easily mounted to trucks or other vehicles as an infantry heavy support weapon.

Eurofighter Typhoon – The Typhoon is a twin-engine, canard-delta wing, multirole fighter. The Typhoon was designed and is manufactured by a consortium of three companies; BAE Systems,

Airbus Group and Alenia Aermacchi, who conduct the majority of affairs dealing with the project through a joint holding company, Eurofighter Jagdflugzeug GmbH, which was formed in 1986. It first flew in March 1994 and was introduced into service in August 2003. The Typhoon is a highly agile aircraft, designed to be an effective dogfighter when in combat with other aircraft; later production aircraft have been increasingly more well-equipped. Powered by Eurojet EJ200 afterburning turbofan, it has a top speed of Mach 2.

Fairchild Republic A10 Thunderbolt II – The A10 or "Warthog" as it is affectionately known, is a twin engine ground attack aircraft, that carries one of the most powerful guns mounted to an aircraft in the form of the 30 mm GAU-8 Avenger cannon. The A10 first flew on the 10 May 1972 and is powered by two General Electric TF34-GE-100A turbofans also used on the S3 Viking. The A10 has proved itself as a formidable ground attack aircraft in both the Iraq and Afghanistan and able to withstand quite a bit of punishment and still fly.

General Atomics MQ-1 Predator – The Predator is a UAV (Unmanned Vehicle) used for reconnaissance of targets and the for battlefield observation. It first flew in July 1994 and powered by a single Rotax 914F turbocharged four-cylinder engine powering a single rear mounted propeller. The MQ-1A has been adapted to carry two AGM-114 Hellfire ATGM or AIM-92 Stinger missiles.

General Dynamics F-16 'Fighting Falcon' – The F-16 is a single engine supersonic, multirole fighter aircraft, developed for the USAF. It first flew in January 1974 and is powered by a single F110-GE-100 afterburning turbofan engine. It is one of the most manoeuvrable aircraft in the world and is used by the U.S. Air Force Thunderbirds display team and has been exported to quite a few air forces around the world.

Heckler & Koch MP7 - The Heckler & Koch MP7 is Personal Defence Weapon manufactured by the German manufacturer Heckler & Koch. It is chambered for the HK 4.6×30mm cartridge. It was originally designed with the new cartridge to meet NATO requirements published in 1989, as these requirements called for a personal defence weapon (PDW) class firearm, with a greater ability to defeat body armour. The MP7 went into production in 2001.

Humvee – The HMMWV (High Mobility Multipurpose Wheeled Vehicle), commonly known as the Humvee, is an American four-wheel drive military vehicle produced by AM General. It has largely supplanted the roles formerly served by smaller Jeeps. It has been in service since 1984 and served in all theatres of war. Powered by an 8 Cylinder. Diesel 6.2 L or 6.5 L V8 turbo diesel and with a top speed of over 70 mph, which drops to 55mph when loaded up to its gross weight. It initially lacked any armour, but later version has had some armour protection added against small arms fire.

Lockheed Martin F-35 Lightning II - is a family of single-seat, single-engine, all weather stealth multirole fighters. The fifth generation combat aircraft is designed to perform ground attack, reconnaissance, and air defence missions. The F-35 has three main models: the F-35A conventional takeoff and landing (CTOL) variant, the F-35B short take-off and vertical-landing (STOVL) variant, and the F-35C carrier-based CATOBAR (CV) variant. It first flew on 15 December 2006, and is still in final development before becoming fully operational. Powered by a single Pratt & Whitney F135 afterburning turbofan it has a top speed of over Mach 1.6.

Lockheed C130 Hercules – The Lockheed C130 Hercules is a four engine turboprop transport aircraft with a high wing design. It first flew in August 1954. Since then there have been many variants used by over 70 countries around the world. Originally powered by four 4 Allison T56-A-15 turboprops. It can carry a payload of around 20,000 kg or up to 92 passengers. It is a highly versatile aircraft and has seen use across the world over its 50 years of continuous service.

North American Rockwell OV-10 Bronco – The Bronco was a twin turboprop light attack and observation aircraft. It was developed in the 1960s as a special aircraft for counter-insurgency (COIN) combat, and one of its primary missions was as a forward air control (FAC) aircraft. It first flew on 16 July 1965 ad was retired in 1995. Powered by two Garrett T76-G-410/412 turboprop, 715hp engines and a top speed of 281 mph.

M16 – The M16 is a lightweight, 5.56 mm, air-cooled, gas-operated, magazine-fed assault rifle, with a rotating bolt, actuated by direct impingement gas operation. The rifle is made of steel, 7075 aluminium alloy, composite plastics and polymer materials. It was developed from the AR-15 and came into service in 1963. The M16 is now the most commonly manufactured 5.56x45 mm rifle in the world. Currently the M16 is in service with more than 80 countries worldwide. It has grown a reputation for ruggedness and reliability and was adopted by the SAS over the less reliable SA80. Later the SAS adopted the C8.

McDonnell Douglas F-4 Phantom II was a tandem two-seat, twin-engine, all-weather, long-range supersonic jet interceptor fighter/fighter-bomber originally developed for the United States Navy. It first flew on and 27 May 1958 entered service in 1960 with the U.S. Navy. Proving highly adaptable, it was also adopted by the U.S. Marine Corps and the U.S. Air Force, and by the mid-1960s had become a major part of their respective air wings. The UK operated the McDonnell Douglas F-4 Phantom II as one of its principal combat aircraft from the 1960s to the early 1990s.

The UK was the first export customer for the Phantom. It differed from the American by being powered by two Rolls-Royce Spey 202/204 low bypass turbofans, with 12,140 lbf dry thrust and 20,500 lbf in afterburner (91.2 kN) each. It had a top speed of Mach 1.9 as a F4M. Being replaced by the Tornado.

McDonnell Douglas F15E 'Strike Eagle' – The F15E Strike Eagle is an all-weather multirole fighter, derived from the McDonnell Douglas (now Boeing) F-15 Eagle. It is powered by two Pratt & Whitney F100-229 afterburning turbofans, 29,000 lbf and capable of Mach 2.5 (2.5 the speed of sound). It first flew in December 1986 and an F15SG version is on order by the ordered by the Republic of Singapore Air Force (RSAF).

Northern Alliance - The Afghan Northern Alliance, officially known as the United Islamic Front for the Salvation of Afghanistan, was a military front that came to formation in late 1996 after the Islamic Emirate of Afghanistan (Taliban) took over Kabul. The United Front was assembled by key leaders of the Islamic State of Afghanistan, particularly president in exile Burhanuddin Rabbani and former Defence Minister Ahmad Shah Massoud.

Panavia Tornado GR4 - The Panavia Tornado is a family of twin-engine, variable-sweep wing combat aircraft, which was jointly developed and manufactured by Italy, the United Kingdom, and West Germany. There are three primary Tornado variants: the Tornado IDS (interdictor/strike) fighter-bomber, the suppression of enemy air defences Tornado ECR (electronic combat/reconnaissance) and the Tornado ADV (air defence variant) interceptor aircraft. The Tornado ADV variant is no longer in RAF service having been retired in 2011, being replaced by the Typhoon. Powered by two Turbo-Union RB199-34R Mk 103 afterburning turbofans and a top speed of Mach 2.2. It has proved to be a very successful aircraft and still in front line service. The Tornado was developed and built by Panavia Aircraft GmbH, a tri-national consortium consisting of British Aerospace (previously British Aircraft Corporation), MBB of West Germany, and Aeritalia of Italy. It first flew on 14 August 1974 and was introduced into service in 1979–1980.

SA80 - The SA80 (Small Arms for the 1980s) is a British family of 5.56mm small arms. It is a selective fire, gas-operated assault rifle. Elements of its design, in particular the bullpup configuration, come from the earlier EM-2 rifle. The first prototypes were trialled in 1976 and production ended in 1994. It is due to remain in service until 2025.

In 2000, Heckler & Koch, at that time owned by the British defence conglomerate BAE Systems, was contracted to upgrade the SA80 family of weapons. 200,000 SA80s were re-manufactured at a cost of £400 each, producing the A2 variant. Changes focused primarily on improving reliability and include: a redesigned cocking handle, modified bolt, extractor and a redesigned hammer assembly that produces a slight delay in the hammer's operation in continuous fire mode, improving reliability and stability.

Sikorsky UH-60 Black Hawk – The UH-60 Black Hawk has been cemented in history after the books and film 'Black hawk down'. It is a four bladed twin engine medium lift helicopter designed for the United States Army. It first flew in October 1974 and has been used in a variety of roles and variants since then. Powered by two General Electric T700-GE-701C turboshaft engines it can carry a variety of payloads and be adapted to suit a wide variety of missions. It was designed from the outset to a high survivability on the battlefield. First being used in combat during the invasion of Grenada in 1983.

Toyota Hilux – The Toyota Hilux is a small pickup truck manufacture by Toyota in Japan. It has been produced since 1968 and is currently on its 7th generation. It can have either front wheel drive or four wheel drive. The Hilux has gained a reputation for exceptional sturdiness and reliability, even during sustained heavy use and/or abuse, and is often referred to as "The Indestructible Truck".

Warrior Tank – The Warrior tank is lightweight tracked vehicle introduced in 1988. It is powered by a Perkins V-8 Condor Diesel engine and a top speed of 46 mph. Armament consists of a 30 mm L21A1 RARDEN cannon, although the 40 mm CTA International CT40 cannon is planned as a future upgrade. Secondary weapons are a L94A1 coaxial 7.62 mm chain gun and a 7.62 mm machine gun. The plan is to upgrade the warrior tanks further to keep them in service until 2025.

Westland Lynx – The Lynx is a British multi-purpose military helicopter that has been in service since 1978 and had its first flight in March 1971. It was the first aerobatic helicopter and still holds the helicopter speed record after being specially modified. Powered by two 2 × Rolls-Royce Gem turboshaft engines, the Lynx has proven itself as a versatile helicopter and quite potent as an attack helicopter. The latest version the Wildcat is due to enter operational service in 2014.

ZSU-23-2 – The ZU-23-2 "Sergey" is a Soviet towed 23 mm anti-aircraft twin-barrelled autocannon. It was designed to engage low-flying targets at a range of 2.5 km as well as armoured vehicles at a range of 2 km and for direct defence of troops and strategic locations against air assault usually conducted by helicopters and low-flying airplanes. Normally, once each barrel has fired 100 rounds it becomes too hot and is therefore replaced with a spare barrel.

APPENDIX – HISTORY OF ZG477

BAe HARRIER GR.9A ZG477
ACCESSION NUMBER X005-5972

Constructed by British Aerospace at Dunsfold as one of 34 new-build Harrier GR.7s, with RR Pegasus 105 turbofan engines and using composite materials with BAe and McDonnell Douglas (US)-built components; following final assembly and flight testing delivered from BAe Dunsfold, Surrey between May 1990 and June 1992; serials batch ZG471 – ZG480. Constructor's Number P67.

Specifications GR7

General characteristics

Length: 46 ft 4 in (14.12 m)

Wingspan: 30 ft 4 in (9.25 m)

Height: 11 ft 8 in (3.56 m)

Wing area: 243 ft² (22.6 m²)

Empty weight: 12,500 lb (5,700 kg)

Loaded weight: 15,703 lb (7,123 kg)

Max. takeoff weight: 18,950 lb VTO, 31,000 lb STO (8,595 kg VTO, 14,061 kg STO)

Powerplant: 1 × Rolls-Royce Pegasus Mk. 105 vectored thrust turbofan, 21,750 lb (96.7 kN)

Performance

Maximum speed: 662 mph (1,065 km/h)

Combat radius: 300 nmi (556 km)

Ferry range: 2,015 mi (3256 km)

Service ceiling: 50,000 ft (15,170 m)

Rate of climb: 14,715 ft/min (74.8 m/s)

Armament

Guns: 2× 25 mm ADEN cannon pods under the fuselage

Hardpoints: 8 (under-wing pylon stations 1A & 7A are intended for air-to-air missiles only) with a capacity of 8,000 lb (3,650 kg) of payload and provisions to carry combinations of:

Rockets: 4× LAU-5003 rocket pods (19× CRV7 70 mm rockets each) or 4× Matra rocket pods (18× SNEB 68 mm rockets each)

Missiles: 6× AIM-9 Sidewinders or 4× AGM-65 Maverick

Bombs: ordnance such as Paveway series of laser-guided bombs, unguided iron bombs (including 3 kg and 14 kg practice bombs)

Other: 2× auxiliary drop tanks or reconnaissance pods (such as the Joint Reconnaissance Pod)

Recce/targetting pods: DJRP, Sniper and TIALD

Air-to-air: AIM-9L Sidewinder

Bombs: Paveway II/III/IV, Enhanced Paveway II/II+, 540 lb and 1000 lb iron bombs.

Air-to-ground: CRV-7 rocket pod, AGM-65 Maverick.

4 Aug 90 Assembly underway; mainplane (s/n 010492) fitted.

28 Aug 90 Entered RAF service as a new aircraft.

Sep 90 Harrier GR.7, with its enhanced night attack operations capability, entered RAF front-line service (with No. 4 Squadron).

5 Nov 90 From BAE Dunsfold to RAF Gutersloh, Germany; airframe hours 5.00.

5 Dec 90 Flown by Malcolm White on Gutersloh on air-to-air training combat mission against Phantoms. Landed at RAF Wittering and returned the following day.

1990/92 With No 4 Squadron, RAF Gutersloh, Germany; aircraft code CC.

1991 All Harrier GR.7s grounded for a period due to teething troubles, mainly

in the electrical system.

27 Aug 92 Gutersloh to RAF St Athan for Phase 4 Modifications; airframe hours

445.50.

1992/93 With No 3 Squadron, RAF Laarbruch, Germany. Aircraft code AK.

8 Dec 92 From No.3 Squadron St Athan to RAF Laarbruch following

modifications; airframe hours 447.00.

8 Apr 93 RAF Laarbruch to Incirlik, Turkey for Operation Warden. Airframe

hours 523.45.

1993/94 With No 4 Squadron, Incirlik, Turkey; aircraft code WI. Following the Kurdish uprising against President Saddam Hussein, in

April 1993 the Harrier Force took over the policing of the Northern Exclusion (No-fly) Zone in Iraq from Jaguar aircraft as part of 'Operation Warden'. Based at Incirlik, the three Harrier squadrons (Nos 1, 3, 4) were rotated on a regular basis until 1995 when this commitment ceased for the Harrier Force.23 Aug 93 Incirlik to RAF Wittering. Airframe hours 722.55.

28 Mar 94 Returned to Incirlik from Wittering. Airframe hours 766.15.

15 Nov 94 Incirlik to RAF Laarbruch, Germany. Airframe hours 1000.50.

10 Jan 97 To BAE Dunsfold.

14 Jul 98 Dunsfold to RAF Laarbruch. Airframe hours 1648.15.

1995/98 Mainly with No 3 Squadron at Laarbruch, Germany as aircraft code '67'

8 Oct 96 To Boscombe Down for Paveway 3 trial.

1999 Based on detachment at Gioia Del Colle, Italy, during Operation Allied

Force in 1999. The Force Objective was 'to degrade and damage the military and security structure that Serbian President Milosevic (Yugoslav President) has used to depopulate and destroy the Albanian majority in the province of Kosovo'. Time of initial attack: 2:00 PM EST, 24 March 1999. Suspension of bombing: 10:00 AM EST, 10 June 1999. Bombing campaign halted: 10:50 AM EST, 20 June 1999.

2000 Became part of newly established Joint Force Harrier, based at RAF Cottesmore, Rutland. Then with No 1 Squadron.

2001-2003 Based with No. 3 Squadron at RAF Cottesmore. Aircraft code 67.

One of 40 new and converted aircraft modified from GR.7 to GR.7A standard with uprated RR Pegasus MK.107 engine from 2003.

29 Jan 2004 To DRA/BAe Systems Warton for conversion (Harrier Maintenance

Programme 3). Airframe hours 3263.55. Upgraded to GR.9A standard. The Harrier GR.9A was the mid-life avionics and weapons update of the GR.7A, some 30 Mk 9As being fitted with the more powerful Pegasus Mk 107, and also a terrain referenced navigation system as part of an Integrated Weapons Programme (IWP).

12 Sep 2005 From BAe Warton to MoD/AFD/QinetiQ at Boscombe Down, Wilts for

trials work. Airframe hours 3267.55.

16 Jun 2006 From Boscombe Down to Cottesmore/Wittering. Airframe hours 3405.15.

20 Jul 06 From Cottesmore/Wittering to Boscombe Down. Airframe hours 3408.50.

6 Mar 07 From Boscombe Down to BAE Warton. Airframe hours 3481.35.20 Apr 07 BAe Systems Warton to Boscombe Down. Airframe hours 3490.02.

20 Dec 07 Boscombe Down to RAF Cottesmore. Airframe hours 3559.25.

Dec 07 Allotted to the Naval Strike Wing, serving with them until February 2008. The Naval Strike Wing was an amalgamation of the two Fleet Air Arm Squadrons, Nos. 800 and 801. (which became 800 Naval Air Squadron on 1 April 2010) Mar-Jun 2008 Undergoing upgrade work (TERMA modification) at Harrier Maintenance Facility (HMF).

Jul 2008 To No 4 Squadron, RAF Cottesmore, on detachment to Afghanistan.

2008/9 Ten months operational service in Afghanistan as part of Operation 'Herrick' from July 2008; squadron code still '67'. Armed for operations with Paveway IV 500lb laser/GPS guided bombs and CRV-7 rocket pods, as well as Digital Joint reconnaissance pods and Sniper Advance Targeting pods. Eight Harriers were continuously available in theatre, with missions flown in pairs, two pairs on day taskings and one pair at night, with other aircraft on alert during the day. The main area of operations was over the Helmand Valley, some 90nm/15-20 minutes flying time from Kandahar, supporting UK Army and Royal Marines as well as other coalition troops. Other areas covered included the Khyber Pass and Pakistan/Iran/Turkmenistan/Uzbekistan border regions.

Jul 09 Joint Force Harrier returned home from its Afghan base at Kandahar. ZG477 had returned home to join No 1 (F) Squadron in June 2009, flying for two months until grounded for servicing.

Aug 2009 Into Stand Alone Minor (SAM) servicing.

31 Mar 10 Last Harrier GR.7s retired, with IV (AC) Squadron disbanded at Cottesmore the same day, leaving only Harrier GR.9 and '9As in service until final retirement. No 20 (R) Squadron at Wittering became IV (R) Squadron to keep the IV nameplate.

Nov 10 Re-allocated to No 1 Squadron following SAM servicing at Cottesmore in preparation for final day of Harrier flying; Given special commemorative livery; red and white tail with No 1 (F) Squadron badge and lettered '1969-2010' on both sides. As the 'Boss Bird', ZG477 was flown by OC No 1 (F) Squadron, Wg Cdr Dave Haines.19 Nov 10 ZG477 was the first of four Cottesmore-based Harriers ('Jedi Flight') embarked towards the end of carrier HMS Ark Royal's final cruise in preparation for farewell departure, as the last Harriers to land on the ship. ZG477 was 'Jedi 1'. Photos – Air Forces Monthly February 2011

24 Nov 10 One of the four aircraft involved in final Harrier departure from a Royal

Navy carrier, from the about-to-be decommissioned aircraft carrier HMS
Ark Royal.
Departure point was in the North Sea east of Newcastle; ZG477 made the
final launch at 09.10hrs, pilot Lt Cdr James 'Blackers' Blackmore.

14 Dec 10 Practice flight by ZG477 and 15 other aircraft ready for the following
day.

15 Dec10 Official 'Farewell to the Harrier' day; End of Joint Force Harrier and of
No. 1 (F) Squadron, and of flying at RAF Cottesmore. Final flight of ZG477; Again as 'Jedi 01' flown in poor weather conditions by Wg Cdr Dave Haines, OC No 1 (F) Squadron, part of the 16-aircraft formation flight and flypast ('Kestrel Formation') from RAF Cottesmore around Lincolnshire and former Harrier bases; grounded following farewell formation flight; all RAF Harriers grounded that day due to defence cuts announced as part of the Strategic Defence Review on 19 October 2010 that included the axing of Joint Force Harrier and UK fleet flagship, HMS Ark Royal. Airframe Hours 4191.25; total landings 3969.

2010/11 Stored serviceable at RAF Cottesmore and regularly ground-run.

2011 Donated to RAF Museum; by road on two low-loaders to Cosford from Cottesmore 19 December 2011, being assembled that day. Moved to MBCC for further work 10 January 2012; placed on public display 30 January 2012.

TEXT; ANDREW SIMPSON

RAF MUSEUM 2012

Printed in Great Britain
by Amazon